MW00335126

MASTERING BUSINESS ANALYSIS STANDARD PRACTICES WORKBOOK

Kelley Bruns, CBAP, PMI-PBA, PMP, PMI-ACP, CSM

Billie Johnson, CBAP, PMI-PBA, CSM

Titles in the

Business Analysis Professional Development Series

This series is for those interested in developing a career in business analysis. Each book within the series will help practitioners develop the knowledge, skills, competencies, and capabilities needed to master the typical business analysis career path. These instructional texts are designed for use in professional training, continuing education courses, and self-learning.

Successful Business Analysis Consulting:
Strategies and Tips for Going It Alone
by Karl Wiegers

Mastering Business Analysis Standard Practices:
Seven Steps to the Next Level of Competency
by Kelley Bruns and Billie Johnson

Mastering Business Analysis Standard Practices Workbook
by Kelley Bruns and Billie Johnson

Seven Steps to Mastering Business Analysis, 2nd Edition
by Jamie Champagne

Mastering Business Analysis Versatility:
Seven Steps to Develop Advanced Competencies and Capabilities
by Gina Schmidt

Agile Business Analysis: Enabling Continuous Improvement
of Requirements, Project Scope, and Agile Project Results
by Kevin Aguanno and Ori Schibi

Copyright © 2019 by J. Ross Publishing

ISBN-13: 978-1-60427-161-4

Printed and bound in the U.S.A. Printed on acid-free paper.

10 9 8 7 6 5 4 3 2 1

This publication contains information obtained from authentic and highly regarded sources. Reprinted material is used with permission, and sources are indicated. Reasonable effort has been made to publish reliable data and information, but the author and the publisher cannot assume responsibility for the validity of all materials or for the consequences of their use.

IIBA, the IIBA logo, *BABOK® Guide*, and Business Analysis Body of Knowledge are registered trademarks owned by International Institute of Business Analysis. CBAP and CCBA are registered certification marks owned by International Institute of Business Analysis. PMI, the PMI logo, PMP, PMI-PBA, and Pulse of the Profession® are all trademarks of Project Management Institute.

All rights reserved. Neither this publication nor any part thereof may be reproduced, stored in a retrieval system, or transmitted in any form or by any means, electronic, mechanical, photocopying, recording or otherwise, without the prior written permission of the publisher.

The copyright owner's consent does not extend to copying for general distribution for promotion, for creating new works, or for resale. Specific permission must be obtained from J. Ross Publishing for such purposes.

Direct all inquiries to J. Ross Publishing, Inc., 300 S. Pine Island Rd., Suite 305, Plantation, FL 33324.

Phone: (954) 727-9333
Fax: (561) 892-0700
Web: www.jrosspub.com

Table of Contents

Introduction

PURPOSE

The purpose of the Mastering Business Analysis Workbook is to provide readers of *Mastering Business Analysis Standard Practices: Seven Steps to the Next Level of Competency* the opportunity to increase their learning by *doing* business analysis work through a fictional, but realistic, case study. This is an excellent opportunity to test your skills. Readers are provided suggested solutions, but keep in mind there are multiple avenues that a business analyst may take to approach the seven steps of achieving business analysis competency.

HOW TO USE THIS GUIDE

The Workbook is designed to be used in conjunction with *Mastering Business Analysis Standard Practices*, such that as each chapter is read there is a corresponding chapter to review in the Workbook. Due to the nature of the case study revealing itself through the "seven steps," it is suggested that you practice using the exercises through the chapters sequentially. However, if you have an immediate gap in your business analysis practice, feel free to read the pertinent chapter and practice your learning with the corresponding Workbook chapter.

The Workbook is divided into the following chapters to align with *Mastering Business Analysis Standard Practices*:

1. Introduction

   This chapter sets the stage for business analysis terminology, roles and responsibilities, the perspectives of business analysis, and business analysis competencies. Before embarking on the business analysis process journey, a depiction of the roadmap for the business analysis process will guide you through the rest of the book.

2. Step 1—Understand Your Stakeholders

   This chapter provides guidance on stakeholder identification and details stakeholder analysis to ensure a thorough understanding before planning or engaging stakeholder involvement.

3. Step 2—Understand the Business Context

   This chapter provides guidance for understanding the organization holistically, performing situational needs analysis, and preparing situational justification for decision makers.

4. Step 3—Plan the Business Analysis Work

    This chapter provides guidance on the areas to be planned for not only the business analysis work effort, but also developing a business analysis communication plan and a business analysis information management plan.

5. Step 4—Set Initiative Scope

    This chapter provides guidance on setting the initiative up for success by developing a clear and concise scope definition boundary.

6. Step 5—Develop Solution Requirements and Design Definition

    This chapter provides guidance on developing the business analysis information that directs the building of the solution to meet stakeholder needs.

7. Step 6—Scope Management

    This chapter provides guidance on maintaining agreement on scope and controlling scope in an ever-changing environment.

8. Step 7—Evaluate Solution

    This chapter provides guidance on the business analysis practitioner's role as the solution is being built and throughout the solution's existence to ensure value continues to be met.

The Appendix contains suggested solutions for the Workbook exercises, providing validation of learning as well as working examples of business analysis tasks and techniques. As you complete each chapter of the Workbook, you will find yourself reaching that next level of business analysis competency. Enjoy the journey!

Introduction to the Case Study: Blue Yonder Insurance Company

Doc-Man Project

BACKGROUND ON YOUR BUSINESS ANALYSIS POSITION

Congratulations! You have secured a position at Blue Yonder Insurance Company to lead the business analysis effort for the Doc-Man Project. During the interview process you have learned that this solution will provide standardized document management practices using a commercial off-the-shelf (COTS) application. You will be reporting to the manager of Enterprise Content Management (ECM), Isabelle Ringing, with a dotted line to the project manager, Neil Down. The project is following an agile framework and a project brief has been written by the project manager. The entire team at this point is made up of:

Product Owner—Abby Normal
Project Manager—Neil Down
Solution Architect—Percy Vere
Change Manager—Joe V. Awl
Project Officer—Willie Findit
Business Analyst—Yourself

All are contractors except Abby Normal who reports to Isabelle Ringing. The existing budget indicates that you will be able to add three additional contract business analysts. You have been given the following to bring yourself up to speed:

- Blue Yonder Company Background—external company website
- Doc-Man Project Brief
- ECM Group Background

Background on Blue Yonder

Blue Yonder is an international insurance services company headquartered in Shermer, IL, USA. The company's main line of business is automobile insurance. Other lines of business include life insurance and property (homeowner, renter, and condo) insurance. Blue Yonder was founded in

1922 by retired jockey, Skye Blue, as a mutual automobile insurance company owned by its policy-holders. The firm initially specialized in auto insurance and later expanded its services into other types of insurance. The company was taken public in 1994 and the Blue family continues to provide leadership for the firm. Currently, Blue Yonder has 65,000 employees and 17,000 agents. Blue Yonder services 80 million policies, of which over 44,000,000 are for automobiles, 27,000,000 are for property, and 9,000,000 are for life.

DOC-MAN PROJECT BRIEF

Executive Summary

The purpose of the Doc-Man Project is to improve Blue Yonder's capability to cost effectively manage its valuable documentation as an integrated enterprise. The primary drivers are to reduce enterprise risk and cost while increasing productivity. This will be achieved by ensuring a single enterprise document management platform for all lines of business. The platform will provide integration services to specialized applications, such as enterprise resource planning tools, and electronic communication to enable attachments and other content to be centrally managed using a common toolset.

A procurement process is currently in progress with a selected vendor to provide the solution as well as integration and ongoing support services. The solution will include a rich set of document management functionalities as well as document workflow to automate business processes, such as claims processing document capture, and enhanced search functionality.

This two-year program of work will prioritize implementation in business areas where the highest value can be realized (e.g., the creation and management of documents to support business operations). The broad scope of implementation across all Blue Yonder's sites is ambitious within a two-year period. To enable this timeframe to be met cost effectively, the project will focus on high-volume, enterprise-wide document creation and management functions only. When the enterprise has migrated to a common platform and decommissioned old platforms, it is expected additional initiatives will be undertaken to leverage supplementary value from the platform.

Program implementation is expected to require an investment of $14.88M over 2.5 years with a contingency of 30%. Governance will be provided by a Steering Committee which will periodically review progress and, if satisfied, approve next stage funding at milestone gates. The Steering Committee will be made up of leaders from the lines of business and support functions.

Background

Abby has led the recent analysis as summarized below:

Timing	Actions
2 years ago	The Term Life Insurance Group was made aware that their existing document management system would no longer be supported. They asked the information technology group to pilot a collaboration tool as a replacement.
1 year ago	The scope was increased to include all life insurance groups and a group was formed to look at the feasibility for a company-wide document management solution. The collaboration tool pilot determined that there was too much risk in using a collaboration tool to manage documents and the decision was made to look for a more robust solution.
Presently	The scope has been increased to support a company-wide document management solution and the Term Life Insurance Group still does not have a document management system replacement. Request for quote has been released to potential vendors and three vendors have been short-listed. The core project team has commenced.

It is also important to look further back to ensure that we are considering what we've already learned. About 10 years ago, Blue Yonder took a run at implementing a company-wide document management solution that was called the Information Administration Project (IAP) and was not successful. We owe it to ask why this program failed and more importantly, "what will we do differently?" The most significant failure was that the business didn't adopt the technology. In the case of IAP, it did not improve nor align with business processes and dictated to the business the conventions they would need to use without understanding the impact.

Doc-Man Project Differences

The first difference is that the Doc-Man Project must be a *business-driven* change with technology partnering with the business leaders to identify areas that would derive the most benefit from a single document management solution. There will be significant investment in each area of the business as they participate, identify their documentation, test, and are trained on the new technology. Additionally, support for continuous improvement and information governance work that goes hand in hand with a technology implementation will take time from a smaller subset of subject matter experts.

The second difference must be the establishment of a platform that is architected loosely into the information ecosystem. The platform must provide the ability to enable required business capabilities. The technology group will shift thinking away from "we will deliver this and you will use it" to a product/platform centric where the users are engaged in the development, product owners prioritize the work, and platform owners deliver the reusable component capabilities. There must be a constant prioritization of the backlog of work in conjunction with the business and an understanding that the platform will be owned and maintained long after the initial deployment is completed. It is not realistic to think that we set up a Doc-Man once and it will manage our documents forever. Rather it will have to continue to evolve as technology evolves. Governance and documentation stewards must be established to ensure the documentation management solution has a long life and evolves even after the initial project to establish the platform is done.

The third key difference is the framework for delivering the solution. An agile approach will allow our users to provide feedback and for adjustments to be made. This should help address one of the biggest challenges with user adoption. As one policy administrator said, "our information is like water, it is going to flow to whatever system is easiest to use." The easiest systems are not generally the ones that include governance, so the challenge is real and we must leverage our new user experience discipline to ensure that this solution is easy to use and widely accepted.

An additional major consideration is the minimization of non-productive or stoppage time for our users as we implement the solution. Much of the documentation is vital to running our business. It is critical that we recognize Blue Yonder cannot afford business disruption associated with the unavailability of documentation.

Summary of Expected Benefits

The following benefits have been defined by the ECM group to obtain funding for the project:

- Reduced global infrastructure and run costs of existing document management systems
- Reduced storage costs
- Reduced integration costs
- Reduced risk of data leakage and increased support for data loss prevention and protection
- Improved personal productivity savings of 885,600 days/year—assumptions based on IDC research which has identified the average information worker spends 2.4 hours/day dealing with document challenges, such as:
  - Searching for but not finding documents
  - Recreating documents that cannot be found
  - Dealing with problems and time-consuming tasks related to the use of paper
- Increased adoption because of a consistent global user experience
- Opportunity for automation of business processes

The 885,600 days/year personal productivity savings assumes only 30% of this study's time can be saved by half of the 82,000 users impacted by the Doc-Man project.

ENTERPRISE CONTENT MANAGEMENT GROUP BACKGROUND

Vision

Employees and agents can access any type of business content within governing regulations and organization guidelines from their digital devices using voice and touch command.

Mission

Enable our people to efficiently manage and access the right information at the right time to enhance productivity and make better decisions.

Guiding Principles

- Our people own their content and are accountable for appropriately managing it
- End-user experience and continuous improvement are key areas of focus
- All Blue Yonder systems' information is managed in accordance with organizational guidelines and governmental regulations for document retention, disposal, or deletion
- ECM leads by example in managing information

Responsibilities of the ECM Group

Service	Definition
CD burning or secure hard drives	Burn and ship a CD/DVD or secure hard drives to offsite storage or to another office, partner, government, or vendor
Disposal of records request	Dispose/destroy documents; verify records have been disposed of with approval; verify legal evidence trail of destroyed records
Document and records management knowledge gathering	Provide consulting services to better understand the user's landscape, current state, unstructured content, and records. Goal is to improve how to leverage tools and increase business productivity
Document production	Generate an inventory of records that meet the scope/requirements of a particular legal discovery
Legal holds to repositories	Preserve all forms of relevant information when litigation is reasonably anticipated
Physical transmittal process	Send/receive electronic or physical data from/to a partner, government, vendor, buyer, or seller
Physical archiving	Manage physical documents in long-term, offsite storage

Current Key Initiatives

- Global Enterprise Content Management Maturity Assessment
- Establish Business Communication Plan utilizing our Technology Business Partners
- Doc-Man Definition Phase
- Initiate Mobile Access to Automobile Policies

Who We Are

The Enterprise Content Management (ECM) group is made up of the following individuals:

- Isabelle Ringing, Manager of ECM group, is accountable for the effective and efficient design, build, deployment, and maintenance of enterprise content management platforms globally to support business productivity and effectiveness in alignment with the overall technology strategy. Isabelle is responsible for leading and developing the ECM Platforms team.
    - Open Position, ECM Change Management, is accountable for the overall communication and training strategies across the ECM and Collaboration portfolio of projects with the objective of providing unified, consistent messaging and tools to the business.
    - Abby Normal, Content Management Supervisor, is accountable for the integration of strong ECM Platform outcomes including integration with Enterprise Applications, Business Applications, and the Technology Partnership team to drive positive outcomes for the business. Abby is responsible for leading and developing the ECM team.
        - ECM Specialists to include Anna Littlical, Norma Leigh Absent, Willie Makit, Lois Di Nominator, Don Messwidme, and Hugo First.
    - Eileen Sideways, Document Governance Supervisor, is accountable for ECM policies, procedures, and document processes to ensure they are efficient, effective, and market leading in alignment with the overall technology strategy. Eileen is responsible for leading and developing the ECM Document Governance team.
        - ECM Document Governance Specialists include Augusta Wind, Anne Teak, Hope Furaletter, Ray O'Sun, and Perry Scope.
    - Saul Goodmate, ECM Platform Delivery Specialist, is accountable for the management of the ECM life cycle that includes the inception, design and delivery, and transition to the run and maintain team to support business productivity and effectiveness in alignment with ECM policy and industry best practices.
    - Carmen Goh, ECM Change and Release Specialist, is accountable for managing the change, release, and configuration process, along with ensuring the standardized processes and procedures are adhered to and embedded throughout technology to protect the live environment and maximize stability for Blue Yonder.
    - Anita Bath, Physical Records Supervisor, is accountable for the security, accessibility, and remediation of all physical records globally to support business productivity and effectiveness in alignment with ECM policy and industry best practice. Anita is responsible for leading and developing the ECM Physical Records team.
        - ECM Physical Records team includes Liz Erd, John Quill, Rosemary Lamb, and Ray Manta.
    - Ray Sin, Deployment Specialist, is accountable for measuring the work intake for ECM and Collaboration.

About the Authors

Kelley Bruns CBAP, CSM, PMI-ACP, PMI-PBA, PMP, ICP, ICP-APM, ICP-BVA

Kelley Bruns is a veteran corporate trainer, coach, mentor, training manager, course developer, and author with more than 25 years of experience helping enterprise project teams solve problems. She holds a Master's degree in Adult Education with a concentration in Training and Development from Drake University. Kelley has facilitated and consulted with participants and clients throughout the world, including corporations, government, and non-profit entities. She is a former Vice President of BA Training at ASPE, and a leading expert in business analysis and various approaches to project management and product development. Kelley is an IIBA Certified Business Analysis Professional (CBAP®), Project Management Institute certified Professional in Business Analysis (PMI-PBA®), Project Management Professional (PMP®), and Agile Certified Practitioner (PMI-ACP®). She is also a Scrum Alliance accredited Certified Scrum Master (CSM) and International Consortium for Agile accredited ICP, ICP-BVA, and ICP-APM.

Kelley has dedicated her career to help people transfer knowledge, skills, and abilities in both professional and personal settings to provide a strong return on investment. Ms. Bruns was actively involved in the IIBA Enhanced Certification Redesign and the Endorsed Education Provider Advisory Group. She is uniquely talented at helping others learn best practices without having to learn the hard way. In her spare time, Kelley can be found hiking, whitewater kayaking, camping, and snowshoeing with her husband and dogs in the mountains near her home.

Billie Johnson, CBAP, PMI-PBA, CSM, IIBA-EEP

Billie Johnson is a leading project management and business analysis expert and practicing professional who has been involved in establishing business analysis direction, processes, and modeling for almost 30 years—spanning the financial, manufacturing, consulting, education, government, retail, and mining industries. She was an early adopter of the IIBA® and Certified Business Analysis Professional™ (CBAP®) certification, receiving her CBAP® certification in May 2007; as well as achieving the Professional in Business Analysis (PMI-PBA)® certification as soon as it was offered in July 2014. She is also a Certified Scrum Master (CSM) accredited by the Scrum Alliance. Billie was a reviewer team lead for the IIBA BABOK Guide® version 3.0. She periodically speaks at International Institute of Business Analysis and Project Management Institute events and other professional conferences. For the last ten years, she has been teaching and consulting with large organizations and Fortune 100 companies. As a business analysis instructor, course developer, author, coach, and mentor, she enjoys furthering the field of business analysis by touching those in the field with tools to face their unique problems and opportunities. In her spare time, Billie and her husband, Craig, enjoy building memories with family and friends at their home on Lake Buchanan in Texas. Very special memories are the Grandmere and Papa camps in the summer with the grandkids.

Chapter 1 Exercises

Introduction

BACKGROUND

This chapter of the Workbook is designed to help you internalize some business analysis concepts discussed in Chapter 1 (Introduction) of *Mastering Business Analysis Standard Practices*.

EXERCISE QUESTIONS

1. How would you summarize the act of doing business analysis?

2. Name at least two values enterprises reap from investing in business analysis.

3. What are the two functions of trust?

4. What are the six business analysis core concepts according to the *Business Analysis Core Concept Model*™?

5. Business analysis is no longer only related to information technology solutions but is performed under other perspectives as well. What were the four other perspectives discussed in Chapter 1?

6. Define the following terms:

    a. Requirement

    b. Design

    c. Business analysis information

7. Is business analysis information always either a requirement or a design?

8. What is the value of decomposing requirements?

9. What are the levels of requirements documented in Chapter 1? Note: you may call these levels by different names in your organization and that's okay, just ensure you are practicing requirements decomposition.

10. Name at least three solution approaches for satisfying requirements and design definitions:

11. Match the term to the definition:

Term	Alpha Match	Definition
User		a. A group or individual with a relationship to the change, the need, or the solution
Software System		b. A set of components (manual, automated, or combination of both) that work together to accomplish a goal
Solution		c. A set of activities designed to accomplish a specific objective by taking one or more defined inputs and turning them into defined outputs
Actor		d. A human, device, or system that plays some specified role in interacting with a solution
Process		e. A stakeholder that interacts with the system and will use the product
Stakeholder		f. Programs that run in the background, enabling applications to function
Application		g. A software program that runs on your computer (e.g., web browsers, e-mail programs, word processors, games, and utilities)
System		h. A specific way of satisfying one or more needs in a context

Chapter 2 Exercises

Step 1: Understand Your Stakeholders

BACKGROUND

The exercises in this chapter will provide you the opportunity to practice stakeholder identification and analysis. The exercises will address these tasks:

- Identify stakeholders
- Analyze stakeholders
- Manage stakeholder collaboration and engagement

These tasks to help understand your stakeholders begin from the moment you first hear of an initiative and continue to be refined throughout the life of the solution. In these exercises, you will practice the initial understanding of Doc-Man stakeholders based on the Blue Yonder Insurance Company Case Study Definition section. So, you will be using Document Analysis for your initial elicitation technique. You will likely have more questions than answers at the end of these exercises.

EXERCISE QUESTIONS

1. Based on the stakeholders that have been defined in the Blue Yonder Insurance Company Case Study Introduction, develop an organizational chart to help you put their roles into perspective (quick reference—Figures 2.4, 2.5, and 2.6, if necessary). Ensure that you document important departments and roles even if you do not have names. Feel free to develop a lower level organizational chart as you deem necessary.

   What questions do you have about the reporting structure?

   What stakeholders do you feel are missing?

Draw the organizational chart here.

2. Begin the Stakeholder Register to start gathering stakeholder identification information.

Stakeholder	Job Position/Role	Dept.	Bldg.	Email	Phone#

3. To begin the analysis of the stakeholders identified in #2, let's quickly plot your perceived Blue Yonder power and impact on the graph below (quick reference—Figure 2.9):

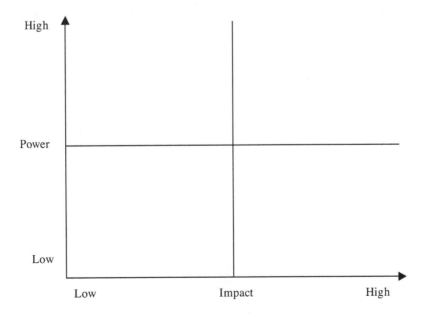

4. The product owner role is critical to ensure a user centric approach. Let's analyze the assigned product owner—Abby Normal. Based on the attributes of a product owner (quick reference—Table 2.3), what are your initial thoughts on the product owner assignment?

Product Owner Assignment	Analysis of Product Owner Assignment
Represents the voice of the domain stakeholders	
Accountable for describing the product vision and product scope so the team understands the direction of the product	
Manages stakeholder expectations by making tough decisions	
Maintains stakeholder relationships and communication with the stakeholders	
Proactively manages and prioritizes the product backlog	
Communicates value proposition and business goals of the product	
Listens and considers the team's input on backlog dependencies	
Spends time with the team and answers their questions	
Defines key product features	
Defines success criteria for the product	
Serves as the single point of contact regarding new requirements and backlog prioritization	
Continuously refines the requirements	
Responsible for the product success and ensuring the product meets the business goals	

Should any of the shortcomings of the product owner be raised and to whom would you suggest?

5. Develop a RACI matrix for the product owner based on the following activities:

Task Responsibilities: R = Responsible (the person who performs the work) A = Accountable (the person who reviews or approves the R's work) C = Consulted (the person(s) who has information to help the R complete work) I = Informed (the person(s) who needs to be notified of the results, but not consulted)	Product Owner— Abby Normal
Approve business analysis deliverables to be delivered	
Inspect and approve requirements (backlog item creation)	
Request and approve changes (backlog management)	
Impact analysis of change of scope requests	
Approve requirements process to be used	
Review and approve requirements traceability structure	
Veto proposed solutions	

6. Managing stakeholder engagement will be an ongoing task throughout the life of the product. Based on your understanding of Chapter 2—Step 1: Understand Your Stakeholders, what initial steps could you take on the Doc-Man project to further stakeholder engagement?

Chapter 3 Exercises

Step 2: Understand the Business Context

BACKGROUND

The exercises in this chapter will provide you the opportunity to use some tools and techniques to better understand the business context Blue Yonder is using to drive the Doc-Man project. If you are new to the industry, organization, or organizational unit(s), you will need to familiarize yourself with those aspects. The exercises will address the following tasks:

- Perform needs analysis
- Define problem/opportunity
- Elicit business analysis information
- Analyze business analysis information
- Obtain consensus

Conducting these tasks prior to defining or selecting a solution will increase the chances for success significantly. The business analyst will continually monitor for any changes in the organizational or industry environment. In reality, this step to understand the business context will flow naturally into Step 4—Set Initiative Scope, perhaps even in the same elicitation event. In our Doc-Man project, you have joined the project after it has been tentatively funded without a formal business case. In these exercises you have been asked to formalize the project for steering-committee approval based on the Doc-Man Project Brief in the Blue Yonder case study information.

EXERCISE QUESTIONS

1. Which of the following business drivers are present for the Doc-Man project (quick reference—Chapter 3: Frequently Identified Business Drivers)? Write a short description of each.

    a. Customer Satisfaction/Customer Impact

   b. Currency

   c. Compliance

   d. Market Position

2. Based on the output of the first question, summarize your needs assessment into one or
    more Situation Statements.

Situation Statement	
The problem or opportunity of . . .	
Has the effect on (of) . . .	
With the impact on (of) . . .	
A successful solution would . . .	

3. Based on the Doc-Man Project Brief, develop a cost benefit analysis (quick reference—Chapter 3: Cost Benefit Analysis section) employing return on investment (assuming 3 years of benefit) as the financial valuation.

4. Develop an informal business case to include the following elements:
   1. Executive Summary
   2. Background
   3. Problem/Opportunity (Needs Assessment)
   4. Benefits/Desired Outcomes
   5. Cost Benefit Analysis
   6. Recommendation

5. The business case will be presented to the Doc-Man Steering Committee. Prepare a force field analysis to support the recommendation.

Forces for Change	Score (1–5)		Forces Against Change	Score (1–5)
		Global Document Management System		
Total			Total	

Chapter 4 Exercises

Step 3: Plan the Business Analysis Work

BACKGROUND

The exercises for this chapter will provide the opportunity to practice business analysis planning using the business analysis planning templates referenced in the text chapters. The exercises will address the following business analysis planning tasks:

- Determine business analysis approach
- Plan business analysis effort
- Plan business analysis governance
- Plan business analysis communication

Each of these tasks require collaboration with stakeholders for consensus and commitment to support the stakeholder engagement level required for Doc-Man's success. The exercises utilize templates introduced in the text, however, feel free to use any other planning tools—provided that you consider the aspects discussed in business analysis planning.

With the initial stakeholder analysis completed, the business context for the insurance industry established, the differentiators Blue Yonder possesses examined, and the basic understanding of the Doc-Man project realized, you are ready to embark on business analysis planning for developing Doc-Man scope definition. After the scope is baselined, you will revisit this chapter for solution requirements and design definitions, along with solution evaluation efforts.

EXERCISES

Scope Definition Planning Exercise Background

Upon joining the Doc-Man project, Percy Vere developed a Doc-Man Solution Architecture Design Document. Lacking a business architecture, Percy developed elements of a business architecture required to reach a solution architecture. In Percy's defense, he was only allowed to engage with a newly formed group of enterprise architects with strictly a technical background. He has also indicated that he expects to use Scrum for the construction and implementation of the solution. In speaking with Percy and Abby, there were user story workshops conducted two years ago with the Term Life Insurance Group that resulted in a 700+ line table of user stories that they feel are appropriate to use as the product backlog and now we just need to start developing the commercial off-the-shelf solution vendor's configuration requirements (transition requirements).

You have a feeling that the user stories provide just a *Life Insurance* view of the functional requirements needed of a document management solution without a Blue Yonder enterprise-wide view of needs and process standardizations required to achieve expected benefits. As you complete the following exercises, remember you are only planning for Doc-Man scope definition:

1. What business analysis approach will you utilize for developing Doc-Man scope definition and why?

2. To begin developing your business analysis activities, focus first on the elicitation and collaboration activities. Using the elicitation and collaboration template below, develop a plan for reaching agreement on the Doc-Man scope definition.

Purpose	Elicitation Technique	Deliverable	Stakeholders	Estimated Dates				Actual Dates			
				Prepare	Conduct	Document	Confirm	Prepare	Conduct	Document	Confirm

3. Based on your elicitation and collaboration activities noted above, complete the table below to derive the level of effort in hours.

Activity	Number of Occurrences	Time Unit (in Hrs)	Total Line Item	Total Category Time
Elicitation and Collaboration: Prepare, Conduct, Confirm, Communicate, and Manage Stakeholders				
Research Techniques				
• Benchmarking and Market Analysis		4		
• Business Rules Analysis		2		
• Data Mining		3		
• Document Analysis		4		
• Interface Analysis		4		
Experiments Techniques				
• Prototyping		12		
• Observation		6		
Collaborative Based Techniques				
• Brainstorming		6		
• Concept Modeling		4		
• Collaborative Games		6		
• Data Modeling		4		
• Focus Groups		12		
• Interviews		4		
• Lessons Learned		4		
• Mind Mapping		4		
• Process Analysis		4		
• Process Modeling		4		
• Survey/Questionnaires		12		
• Requirements Workshop		72		

4. Complete the following table to define the activities to analyze the results of the elicitation and collaboration activities and to develop the scope definition documentation.

Activity	Number of Occurrences	Time Unit (in Hrs)	Total Line Item	Total Category Time
Requirements Analysis and Design Definition: Define Requirements Architecture, Specify and Model Requirements, Verify and Validate Requirements, Define Design Options (recommend solution), and Analyze Potential Value. *Consider Transition Requirement Development as well.*				
Establish Requirements Architecture		5		
Specify and Model Requirements				
People and Roles Modeling Techniques				
• Organizational Modeling		8		
• Roles and Permissions Matrix		12		
• Stakeholder List, Map or Personas		12		
Rationale Modeling Techniques				
• Decision Modeling		3		
• Scope Modeling		8		
• Business Model Canvas		8		
• Root Cause Analysis		4		
• Business Rules Analysis		5		
Activity Flow Modeling Techniques				
• Event-Response Tables		4		
• Process Modeling		6		
• Use Cases		6		
• User Stories		1		
Capability Modeling Techniques				
• Business Capability Analysis		6		
• Functional Decomposition		4		
• Prototyping		6		
Data and Information Modeling Techniques				
• Data Modeling		4		
• Data Dictionary and Glossary		4		
• Data Flow Diagrams		3		
• Glossary		4		
• State Diagrams		6		
• Interface Analysis		4		
Non-Functional Requirements Analysis		6		

Continued

Activity	Number of Occurrences	Time Unit (in Hrs)	Total Line Item	Total Category Time
Compile Requirements and Design Documentation				
• Product Roadmap		6		
• Vision Document		6		
• Product Backlog		8		
• Business Requirements Document (BRD)		8		
• Software/System Requirements Specification (SRS)		8		
• Vendor Selection documents (RFI, RFP, RFQ)		8		
• Model developed to extract packages		1		
Verification and Validation Iterative Reviews				
Verification of Requirements		2		
Validation of Requirements		2		
Prioritization of Requirements				
Prioritization Sessions - Techniques				
• MoSCoW (Must, Should, Could, Won't)		3		
• Voting		3		
• Timebox/Budgeting		3		
• Acceptance and Evaluation Criteria		3		

5. Complete the business analysis communication plan template below to achieve stakeholder engagement for developing Doc-Man scope definition.

Who (Target Audience)	What (Information Needed by the Target Audience)	When		How (Method or Channel)	By Whom (Who Provides)
		Timing	Frequency		

6. Develop the business analysis information governance plan for the Doc-Man scope definition using the template below.

Requirement Management Component	Description		Location	Established?
Repository	*Description of Repository*			
Traceability Architecture	*Description of Traceability Architecture*			
Requirement Attributes	**Unique Identifier:** Ideally, system generated identification of requirement that is never reused.	Field Values		
	Author: This attribute may be tracked by the tool; however, if not, this attribute provides reference for clarification if the requirement is later found to be ambiguous.			
	Ownership: Indicates the business owner after release to the target environment. Provides guidance on who to consult if trade-offs or negotiation are required as well.			
	Source: Provides who has the authority to define the requirement. Subsequently, this source must be consulted of requirement changes and provide more information regarding the requirement if necessary or to justify the need.			
	Urgency: Indicates when the requirement will be needed.			
	Priority: Aids in analysis focus, solution selection, and allocation.			
	Revision Number: Aids in tracking the requirement changes.			
	Status: Indicates the completion status of the requirement. Consider using values such as Proposed, Accepted, Verified, Postponed, Canceled, or Implemented.			
	Notes: Provides information that is not requirements and is intended to be used sparingly.			
Requirement Prioritization Process	*Description of Requirement Prioritization Process*			
Change Management Process	*Description of Change Management Process*			
	Description of Change Request			
	Reference "Stakeholder Responsibilities" for change request authorization, impact analysis, and change authorization.			

Solution Requirements, Design Definition, and Solution Evaluation Planning Background

As you near the finish line of completing the Doc-Man scope definition baseline, you will likely be developing or refining solution requirements, design definition, and solution evaluation activities. The roll-out strategy involves providing the highest value functionality one line of business or supporting function at a time. Even though it has taken some convincing, the project team stakeholders have finally agreed that requirements will be developed iteratively and just-in-time as the project team (consisting of our Blue Yonder core team and the vendor's team) tackles the user stories for upcoming sprints rather than requiring all the details up front. The project team will be co-located in a collaborative workspace. The exercises below should be completed after finishing the Chapter 5 Exercises. As you complete the exercises below, keep in mind that you will be planning for elaboration of the highest priority requirements to be implemented for an iteration.

1. What business analysis approach should be utilized for elaborating solution requirements?

2. To begin developing your business analysis activities, focus first on the elicitation and collaboration activities. Using the elicitation and collaboration template below, develop a plan for reaching agreement on the Doc-Man solution requirements and design definition.

Purpose	Elicitation Technique	Deliverable	Stakeholders	Estimated Dates				Actual Dates			
				Prepare	Conduct	Document	Confirm	Prepare	Conduct	Document	Confirm

3. Based on your elicitation and collaboration activities noted above, complete the table below to derive the level of effort in hours.

Activity	Number of Occurrences	Time Unit (in Hrs)	Total Line Item	Total Category Time
Elicitation and Collaboration: Prepare, Conduct, Confirm, Communicate, and Manage Stakeholders				
Research Techniques				
• Benchmarking and Market Analysis		4		
• Business Rules Analysis		2		
• Data Mining		3		
• Document Analysis		4		
• Interface Analysis		4		
Experiments Techniques				
• Prototyping		12		
• Observation		6		
Collaborative Based Techniques				
• Brainstorming		6		
• Concept Modeling		4		
• Collaborative Games		6		
• Data Modeling		4		
• Focus Groups		12		
• Interviews		4		
• Lessons Learned		4		
• Mind Mapping		4		
• Process Analysis		4		
• Process Modeling		4		
• Survey/Questionnaires		12		
• Requirements Workshop		72		

4. Complete the following table to define the activities to analyze the results of the elicitation and collaboration activities and to develop the solution requirements and design definition documentation.

Activity	Number of Occurrences	Time Unit (in Hrs)	Total Line Item	Total Category Time
Requirements Analysis and Design Definition: Define Requirements Architecture, Specify and Model Requirements, Verify and Validate Requirements, Define Design Options (recommend solution), and Analyze Potential Value. *Consider Transition Requirement Development as well.*				
Establish Requirements Architecture		5		
Specify and Model Requirements				
People and Roles Modeling Techniques				
• Organizational Modeling		8		
• Roles and Permissions Matrix		12		
• Stakeholder List, Map or Personas		12		
Rationale Modeling Techniques				
• Decision Modeling		3		
• Scope Modeling		8		
• Business Model Canvas		8		
• Root Cause Analysis		4		
• Business Rules Analysis		5		
Activity Flow Modeling Techniques				
• Event-Response Tables		4		
• Process Modeling		6		
• Use Cases		6		
• User Stories		1		
Capability Modeling Techniques				
• Business Capability Analysis		6		
• Functional Decomposition		4		
• Prototyping		6		
Data and Information Modeling Techniques				
• Data Modeling		4		
• Data Dictionary and Glossary		4		
• Data Flow Diagrams		3		
• Glossary		4		
• State Diagrams		6		
• Interface Analysis		4		
Non-Functional Requirements Analysis		6		

Continued

Activity	Number of Occurrences	Time Unit (in Hrs)	Total Line Item	Total Category Time
Compile Requirements and Design Documentation				
• Product Roadmap		6		
• Vision Document		6		
• Product Backlog		8		
• Business Requirements Document (BRD)		8		
• Software/System Requirements Specification (SRS)		8		
• Vendor Selection documents (RFI, RFP, RFQ)		8		
• Model developed to extract packages		1		
Verification and Validation Iterative Reviews				
Verification of Requirements	1	2		4
Validation of Requirements	1	2	2	
Prioritization of Requirements				
Prioritization Sessions - Techniques				
• MoSCoW (Must, Should, Could, Won't)		3		3
• Voting		3		
• Timebox/Budgeting		3		
• Acceptance and Evaluation Criteria	1	3	3	

5. Complete the table below to define the activities and the estimated level of effort for solution evaluation.

Activity	Number of Occurrences	Time Unit (in Hrs)	Total Line Item	Total Category Time
Solution Evaluation: Measure Solution Performance, Analyze Performance Measures, Assess Solution Limitations, Assess Enterprise Limitations, and Recommend Actions to Increase Solution Value				
Assess Solution Limitations and Recommend Actions to Increase Solution Value				
Participate in assessing solution options		2		
Participate in allocating requirements to solution components/iterations		2		
Assess Enterprise Limitations				
• Cultural Assessment		4		
• Operational or Technical Assessment		4		
• Stakeholder Impact Analysis		4		
Measure Solution Performance and Analyze Performance Measures				
Attend test case reviews		2		
Address test inquiry/defect resolution		6		
Attend design reviews		2		
Address development inquiries		6		
Change request impact analysis		2		
Complex implementation support		12		

6. Complete the business analysis communication plan template below to review with stakeholders. This is designed to seek stakeholder engagement commitment for developing Doc-Man solution requirements and design definition.

Who (Target Audience)	What (Information Needed by the Target Audience)	When		How (Method or Channel)	By Whom (Who Provides)
		Timing	Frequency		

7. Develop the business analysis information governance plan for Doc-Man solution requirements and design definition using the template below.

Requirement Management Component	Description		Location	Established?
Repository	*Description of Repository*			
Traceability Architecture	*Description of Traceability Architecture*			
Requirement Attributes	**Unique Identifier:** Ideally, system generated identification of requirement that is never reused.	Field Values		
	Author: This attribute may be tracked by the tool; however, if not, this attribute provides reference for clarification if the requirement is later found to be ambiguous.			
	Ownership: Indicates the business owner after release to the target environment. Provides guidance on who to consult if trade-offs or negotiation are required as well.			
	Source: Provides who has the authority to define the requirement. Subsequently, this source must be consulted of requirement changes and provide more information regarding the requirement if necessary or to justify the need.			
	Cost: Associated monetary amount for implementation, maintenance, and/or those borne by others.			
	Stability: Indicates the maturity of the requirement signaling the implementation SMEs if the requirement is firm enough to begin work. This provides an indicator of requirements' doneness.			
	Urgency: Indicates when the requirement will be needed.			
	Priority: Aids in analysis focus, solution selection, and allocation.			
	Resource Assignment: Aids in determining the resources required for elaboration of the requirement. This may include BAs, Domain SMEs, Implementation SMEs, etc.			
	Revision Number: Aids in tracking the requirement changes.			
	Complexity: Indicates the difficulty of implementation (you may use a measure such as number of interfaces, complexity of processes, or number of resources)			
	Status: Indicates the completion status of the requirement. Consider using values such as Proposed, Accepted, Verified, Postponed, Canceled, or Implemented.			
	Notes: Provides information that is not requirements and is intended to be used sparingly.			

Continued

Requirement Management Component	Description	Location	Established?
Requirement Prioritization Process	*Description of Requirement Prioritization Process*		
Change Management Process	*Description of Change Management Process*		
	Description of Change Request		
	Reference "Stakeholder Responsibilities" for change request authorization, impact analysis, and change authorization.		

Chapter 5 Exercises

Step 4: Set Initiative Scope

BACKGROUND

The exercises for this chapter will provide the opportunity to practice developing an initiative scope definition using tools and techniques (Table 5.2 provides a quick reference) gained from reading Chapter 5 in the text. The exercises will address the following business analysis scope development tasks (Table 5.1 provides a quick reference):

- Elicit business analysis information
- Analyze business analysis information
- Collaborate business analysis information
- Obtain consensus

Each of these tasks require collaboration with stakeholders for Doc-Man scope definition consensus. With the initial stakeholder analysis completed, a business context for the insurance industry established, a basic understanding of the differentiators Blue Yonder possesses and the Doc-Man project, and the business analysis planning agreed upon, you are ready to embark on developing Doc-Man scope definition.

During the review of the Business Analysis Communication Plan for Doc-Man scope definition, the business leaders and business technology partners were not overly excited about providing time for a document management solution even though they agreed that their business would be crippled if documents were not managed appropriately. The Term Life Group has the immediate need and feel that a lot of effort was put into user story writing workshops. They feel that these stories are probably typical of the entire organization and they are adamant that this work should be utilized in the scoping effort. They want to understand the benefits and constraints for this project, but agreed to provide resources as needed by the plan set forward.

EXERCISE QUESTIONS

1. As just mentioned, the business leaders and business technology partners want to understand more about the project. That typically means understanding what's in it for them. Based on the Doc-Man Project Brief, develop material (the benefits) that you can use in the eight interviews planned with these stakeholders to seek confirmation of their expectations.

2. Before engaging the stakeholders and according to the Business Analysis Plan for scope definition, you have reviewed the hundreds of user stories that were derived from user story writing workshops with the Term Life Insurance Group about two years ago and have developed the following themes:

   - Manage Documents
   - Search Documents
   - Manage Document Retention
   - Perform Analysis
   - Administer Doc-Man

   Develop a visualization of these themes that may be used for your own understanding as you move into the workshops.

3. You have a two-day workshop coming up with trusted decision makers from the lines of business and support functions. In the workshop, you are likely to employ many techniques. How will you tackle defining the following elements to define Doc-Man scope in an engaging fashion?

    -   Prioritized Doc-Man expected benefits

    -   Barriers for an enterprise-wide document management solution

    -   Developing a common terminology

    -   Who (human and non-human) uses a document management solution at Blue Yonder

    -   What they do with the solution

4. Based on your plan in Exercise #3, develop the workshop outputs of each of the elements. If you are working alone, you can just make up the expected outcome. If you have a group, assign line of business and support function decision maker roles and have fun with the role playing.

    - Prioritized expected Doc-Man benefits:

    - Barriers to an enterprise-wide document management solution:

    - Developing a common terminology:

    - Who (human and non-human) uses a document management solution at Blue Yonder and what they do with the solution

5. Develop the Doc-Man Scope definition using the following template. If you feel there are sections that are not applicable, feel free to remove or add sections as well. As you use this to analyze (make sense out of) the workshop output, you will likely have questions. Follow-up with the applicable workshop participants for direction.

Doc-Man Project

SCOPE DEFINITION DOCUMENT

| Date | Doc-Man Project |

Note: Text written in this document is intended as an aid to the author and should be deleted before this document is released. Update the title and project name by updating the Word Doc properties. The purpose of the document is to ensure all stakeholders agree on what problem they are attempting to solve.

BLUE YONDER   Introduction

Definitions

This section should include any terminology that will be used in this document.

Term	Definition

BLUE YONDER   Introduction

Version History

This section should be used to track changes to the document.

Date	Description of Change	Author	Version

Endorsement/Approval History

This section should include any endorsements and approvals of the document throughout the life of the project.

Timing	Responsibility	Responsible Parties	Confirmation

1   Introduction

Purpose of Document

This section should include a short summary of the objectives that the system will achieve by the end of the project lifecycle.

Document Audience

This section should describe the stakeholders that will use this document.

Reference Documentation

This section should include any terminology that will be used in this document.

No	Title	Author	Location

BLUE YONDER   Doc-Man Project

2   Doc-Man Purpose

Business Opportunity

This section should include a short paragraph to describe the project's value to the organization. What untapped opportunity or unsolved problem does the system address? Can this opportunity be quantified?

Project Objectives

This section should include a list of at least three key strategic objectives.

Vision Statement

This section should include a one-sentence vision statement for the project that all stakeholders can keep foremost in their minds.

Problem Statements

This section includes three problem statement tables.

1) The problem of

Affects

The impact of which is

*A successful solution
would*

2) The problem of

Affects

The impact of which is

*A successful solution
would*

3) The problem of

Affects

The impact of which is

*A successful solution
would*

3   Benefits

This section should include business benefits envisioned by users and explain why the project is being undertaken.

4   Stakeholders

This section should include a list of stakeholder classifications for the project.

Stakeholder Classification

Stakeholder Type	Description	Engagement Classification	Membership

BLUE YONDER   Stakeholders

Personas

This section should include a list of personas to represent fictional but realistic users. Elaborate one of the personas in detail.

Name   Role   Background   Needs   Valued Features

5   Stakeholder Requirements

This section should include stakeholder requirements, which are imprecise by their very nature and not intended to be used to build/configure a solution. These requirements convey the high-level needs of the stakeholders and what they require from the solution. The implementation of these requirements will help to realize the benefits stated previously and will ultimately allow the objectives to be met, business benefits envisioned by users, and explain why the project is being undertaken. Use the sections below as suggestions for depicting stakeholder requirements.

BLUE YONDER   Stakeholder Requirements

5.1 Interactions Depicted by Context Diagram

BLUE YONDER   Stakeholder Requirements

5.2 Actor Generalization Diagram

BLUE YONDER   Stakeholder Requirements

5.3 Epic Stories Diagram

BLUE YONDER   Stakeholder Requirements

5.3.1 Epic Story Briefs ("Epic Story" defined in Definitions)

5.4 Data Requirements

Likely a conceptual data model and state diagram for that all-important business object.

5.4.1 Conceptual Data Model

BLUE YONDER   Stakeholder Requirements

5.4.2 Document State Diagram

BLUE YONDER   Stakeholder Requirements

5.5 Non-Functional Requirements

PERFORMANCE:
Response Time

CAPACITY & SCALABILITY:
Concurrent Users

AVAILABILITY:

LOCALIZATION:

RELIABILITY:

RECOVERABILITY:

OPERABILITY:
Ease of Use

SECURITY:
Data Classification

System Access

Audit

COMPATIBILITY:
Integration

5.6 External Interface Requirements

Describe any requirements or constraints the external environment places on the system. For example, are there any time constraints that must be met?

BLUE YONDER   Stakeholder Requirements

5.7 Business Rules

Describe any definitional or behavioral business rules that will impact the project.

6   Risk Register

ID	Description	Likelihood	Impact	Risk Response (Avoid, Reduce, Fallback, Transfer, Share, or Accept)

7   Appendix A: Stakeholder Review Attendees

Name of Attendee	Role of Attendee

NOTE: This blank Attendee Register is a reminder to have a record of the attendance. The review requires attendance from a Domain SME, Implementation SME, and Tester for verification and validation.

6. The workshop technique that you employed allowed for elicitation and collaboration to occur on a real-time basis for most of the scope definition. During the development of the Doc-Man Scope Definition Document, you have sought out clarification and deferred decisions to reach a collaborative result. It is now time to confirm the results. Consider the following to plan for the Doc-Man scope review:

   - What communication vehicle will you use for the review?

   - How long in advance should you send out the Doc-Man Scope Definition Document to the reviewers?

   - How do you expect the reviewers to prepare for the review?

   - Develop the communication to the reviewers to set expectations.

Chapter 6 Exercises

Step 5: Develop Solution Requirements and Design Definition

BACKGROUND

The exercises for this chapter provide the opportunity to practice developing solution requirements and design definition for the first iteration of Doc-Man sprints using tools and techniques gained from reading Chapter 6 in the text (Table 6.6 provides a quick reference). The exercises will address the following solution requirement and design definition tasks (Table 6.1 provides a quick reference):

- Elicit business analysis information
- Analyze business analysis information
- Collaborate business analysis information
- Obtain consensus

Each of these tasks require collaboration with stakeholders for Doc-Man solution definition consensus. With the Doc-Man scope definition baselined, you have completed the business analysis planning for solution requirements and design definition, and you have the information governance plan established. Now, further elaboration of the product backlog can commence.

The Term Life Insurance Group will be the first business area in which Doc-Man will be rolled out as their current document management system will no longer be supported. Based on the scope workshop output, the Search Documents epic story and supporting business rules were of highest priority. Based on the feedback from the Term Life group, you and the product owner will be utilizing the output from previous user story writing workshops (conducted two years ago) to elaborate user stories (from the bottom up). They are adamant that this work should be utilized in the solution requirements effort, even though you realize that the world does not stand still for two years and the business analysis information derived will need to be validated and likely further elaborated.

EXERCISE QUESTIONS

1. The first step in eliciting solution level requirements is to understand the as-is state. The suggested plan is to utilize observation and interface analysis to achieve this understanding.

In preparing for these two elicitation activities, develop a list of questions that you want to get answered.

a. Observation:

b. Interface analysis:

2. Based on the Doc-Man scope definition from the previous chapter, the epic stories were summarized although not in a true story format. Visualizations bring this information to life. Develop a visualization (theme diagram) of each epic story to decompose these into themes.

    a. Search Documents:

    b. Manage Documents:

   c. Manage Retention:

   d. Administer Doc-Man:

    e. Perform Analysis:

3. In the scope definition in the previous chapter, the Search Content epic story was the highest priority. Based on the Search Content themes developed in the previous question, you are working with the product owner and Term Life SMEs to:

    a. Determine the highest priority *Search Content* theme:

    b. Decompose that highest priority *Search Content* theme into user stories using the template below:

User Story Name	As a . . .	I need to . . .	So that . . . .

c. Develop acceptance criteria for three of those user stories using the template below:

User Story Name	Acceptance Criteria

4. In preparation for the sprint planning session, you must consider what data will need to be defined, what business rules must be explained, and the external interfaces and non-functional items that must be considered. These data definitions, business rules, external interfaces, and non-functional requirements are likely to be reused by other user stories and candidates for requirements to be maintained long after the solution team is gone. Even in an agile environment, lightweight documentation can provide high value. Select one of the user stories above and elaborate the acceptance criteria further with these types of requirements. You may determine that you have a specific business rule buried in the acceptance criteria that you want to be able to reference in other user stories. This may also bring to light opportunities for story splitting if required by the project team.

   a. User story name:
   b. Data definition (use the template below):

Data Definition Identifier DD–XX	Associated Business Object	Data Attribute	Description	Field Type	...

AND/OR further flesh out the conceptual data model.

c. Business rules (use the template below):

Business Rule Identifier BR–XX	If . . .	Then . . .	Else (optional) . . .

AND/OR further flesh out rules in a decision matrix, state diagram, etc.

d. External interface requirements (use the template below):

External Interface EI–XX	Description

OR just draw it:

e. Non-functional requirements (use the template below):

Nonfunctional Identifier NFR–XX	Description

5. With the product owner and project team, utilize the real options technique to determine backlog management required; specifically, removal from the backlog, prioritized differently in the backlog, decomposed further in the backlog, or moved to the sprint backlog. Once moved to the sprint backlog, the backlog item is committed. Consider the three user stories you have elaborated in this exercise. Explain the results below.

Chapter 7 Exercises

Step 6: Manage Scope

BACKGROUND

The exercises for this chapter provide the opportunity to practice tasks involved in managing scope for the first iteration of Doc-Man sprints using tools and techniques gained from reading Chapter 7 in the text (Table 7.2 provides a quick reference). The exercises will address the following manage scope tasks (Table 7.1 provides a quick reference):

- Verify requirements
- Validate requirements
- Recommend solutions
- Monitor product requirements and design definition
- Scope change

Since the Doc-Man project is utilizing an agile framework, these tasks will be performed in a less formal fashion; however, they are still required to ensure consensus that drives user adoption. With the Doc-Man scope definition baselined, you have the information governance plan established and have elaborated the highest priority backlog items in the form of traced user stories. Now, the verification and validation of the product backlog can commence.

EXERCISE QUESTIONS

1. Which task should be performed first—verification or validation—and why?

2. Using the INVEST principle, describe your suggested approach to verification of one user story you elaborated with acceptance criteria in the previous workbook chapter.

3. Abby Normal has mentioned that the user rights definition is under review. What would you suggest for validating the business rules that have been elicited and analyzed in association with searching documents?

4. Blue Yonder has many platforms and applications that house all types of documents. Blue Yonder was in a position to select one of their current applications and roll it out globally or look for other vendors that provide additional functionality. The buzz going around was that the chosen vendor had seamless AI (artificial intelligence) that would make it easy for the users to save their valuable information and not worry about all the metadata tagging. Blue Yonder entered into a tentative agreement based on a successful prototype with the Term Life Insurance Group. The current sprint theme is "Retrieve Search Results." It has become apparent that in setting up the documents to have something to retrieve, the ECM team will be burdened with maintaining a time-consuming and complex management of business rules to make the AI capability seamless to the contributor role. In your research, you have discovered that 60% of the company has some instance of a common application. What type of analysis(es) should you perform to help make the best decision?

5. During the sprint, the team (including yourself) have mocked up the configuration of the summary screen. What should you do with this artifact?

6. The prototype has been impressive; however, it has been determined that the new vendor's product does not provide any additional capabilities than the product being used in house (inconsistently). With the results of the prototype and analysis performed in question 4, you have reviewed with Isabelle Ringing (the sponsor) and determined to renew the COTS solution owned already, but standardized globally. What changes for your business analysis information?

Chapter 8 Exercises

Step 7: Evaluate the Solution

BACKGROUND

The exercises for this chapter provide the opportunity to consider solution evaluation tasks using tools and techniques gained from reading Chapter 8 in the text (Table 8.2 provides a quick reference). The exercises will address the following solution evaluation tasks (Table 8.1 provides a quick reference):

- Provide solution design feedback
- Requirement allocation support
- Solution team support
- Monitor and evaluate the solution

Utilizing an agile framework for the Doc-Man project supports business involvement through the product owner and the BA. As the iterations of sprints are implemented to production, there is an opportunity to monitor for continual improvement.

To set the stage, the sprint planning is complete and product backlog items have moved to the sprint backlog. This sprint's theme will be to provide Search Functionality for documents that reside in Doc-Man for the Term Life Insurance Group.

EXERCISE QUESTIONS

1. Percy Vere and the Vendor's Solution Architect, Soledad Grounds, are at odds regarding the design of the interface and document source of truth for BLUE YONDER's collaborative workspace applications. Soledad's suggested technical design is to manage the documents safely in Doc-Man; however, the Contributor will only be able to access through a collaborative workspace. The Contributor will be responsible for consciously making the decision to publish to Doc-Man and indicate major and minor version updates. Percy maintains that the single source of truth should be the Doc-Man solution, but sees the value of working in a tool built for collaboration until the document is of business value and should be managed. How would you provide feedback to this situation?

2. The sprint backlog has been committed by utilizing the real options technique to support user story commitment, leaving some options open on the product backlog in the previous chapter. You have intentionally avoided developing process models that would dictate a specific flow of the process due to the solution approach of buying a packaged solution (commercial off-the-shelf). Rather, you have identified the goals through user stories and acceptance criteria with reusable data definitions, business rules, external interface, and non-functional requirements. You heard multiple times (in workshops, observation sessions, interviews) that the current system "does not *get* me." So, the solution is designed out of the box such that the requirements to understand the user's business context are the responsibility of the user rather than the system interpreting the user's business context from their derived profile. How would you approach this requirement allocation?

3. You and the product owner, Abby Normal, have been asked to provide feedback on constructed functionality to enter metadata search criteria. What would you expect the project team member to provide and what would you expect to do with that information?

4. What technique could you employ or suggest utilizing at the sprint review to ensure each sprint backlog item is complete and why?

5. The Doc-Man Project has gone through multiple iterations and the Term Life Insurance Group is "live" with the core functionality defined in the most recent version of Doc-Man scope definition.

   a. How will you ensure that the solution is delivering expected value and maintains that level of value in the future?

b. How will you monitor for opportunities to improve on the value that Doc-Man delivers?

Appendices

(Exercise Solutions)

Chapter 1
Exercise Sample Solutions

1. Business analysis is the set of activities to enable change in an enterprise by defining needs and recommending solutions that deliver continuous value to stakeholders.

2. The value enterprises reap by investing in business analysis can be summarized as:

    - Solutions that meet stakeholder needs and provide business value due to more reliable, higher quality requirements
    - Higher buy-in for the change by ensuring stakeholder engagement in the process
    - Projects are more likely to be delivered on time, within scope, and within budget
    - Reusable pattern on future change initiatives by building business analysis competency

3. The two functions of trust are character and competence.

4. The six business analysis core concepts according to the *Business Analysis Core Concept Model*™ are:

    - Change: going through a transformation in response to a need
    - Need: problem or opportunity that requires being addressed
    - Solution: specific way to satisfy one or more needs
    - Stakeholder: group or individual; have a relationship to the change, need, or solution
    - Value: worth, importance, or usefulness to a stakeholder, considering the context
    - Context: circumstances which influence, are influenced by, and provide understanding regarding the change

5. Business analysis perspectives from Chapter 1 other than IT include:

    a. Business Intelligence
    b. Business Process Management
    c. Business Architecture
    d. Agile

6. Definitions of:

    a. Requirement—usable representation of a need
    b. Design—usable representation of a solution
    c. Business analysis information—comprises all of the information business analysts elicit, create, compile, and disseminate in the course of performing business analysis. It is any kind of information at any level of detail that is used as an input to business analysis work or an output of business analysis work.

7. No, business analysis information could be meeting minutes, planning, etc.

8. Here are some examples of value derived from decomposing requirements:

    a. Focus is placed on the level expected for the output
    b. Ensures a clear understanding of problem and scope before the nitty gritty details
    c. Enables traceability back to goals
    d. Without these levels and types of requirements, the BA is less confident that a thorough analysis is complete for the purpose and timing

9. Requirement levels:

    a. Business requirements
    b. Stakeholder requirements
    c. Solution requirements
    d. Transition requirements

10. Solution approaches:

    a. Build
    b. Buy
    c. Combination of Build and Buy
    d. Process Improvement
    e. Organizational Structure Redesign

11. Term Matching:

Term	Alpha Match	Definition
User	E	a. A group or individual with a relationship to the change, the need, or the solution
Software System	F	b. A set of components (manual, automated, or combination of both) that work together to accomplish a goal
Solution	H	c. A set of activities designed to accomplish a specific objective by taking one or more defined inputs and turning them into defined outputs
Actor	D	d. A human, device, or system that plays some specified role in interacting with a solution
Process	C	e. A stakeholder that interacts with the system and will use the product
Stakeholder	A	f. Programs that run in the background, enabling applications to function
Application	G	g. A software program that runs on your computer (e.g., web browsers, e-mail programs, word processors, games, and utilities)
System	B	h. A specific way of satisfying one or more needs in a context

Chapter 2
Exercise Sample Solutions

Step 1: Understand Your Stakeholders

EXERCISE SAMPLE SOLUTIONS

1. You may have used any of the three organizational models (divisional/market, functional, or matrix). This sample solution here depicts the divisional/market based on the information we have at this point. Preparing this model will help you consume the organization's structure to fill in the gaps and question any differences perceived versus documented.

Perceived Blue Yonder Organizational Structure

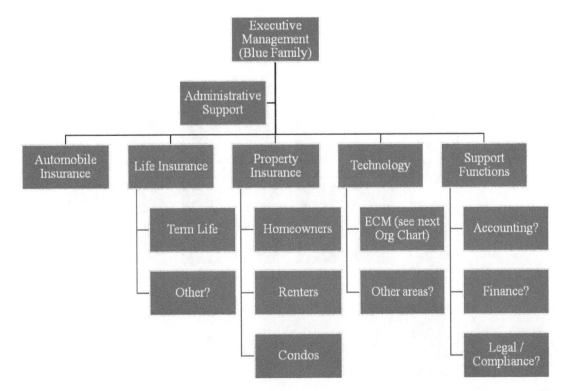

Perceived Enterprise Content Management (ECM) Structure

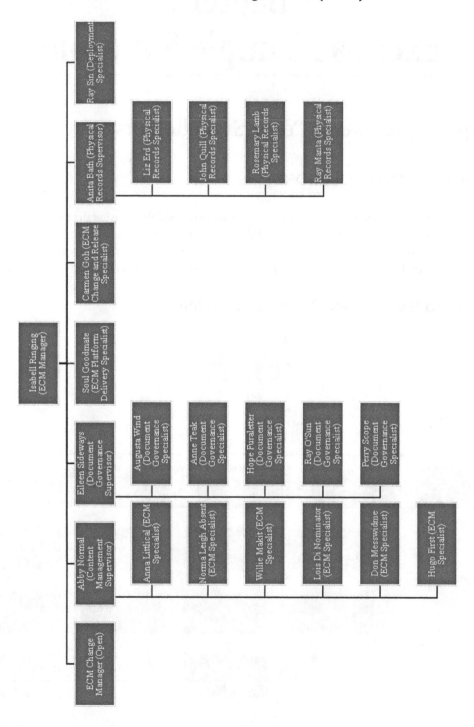

Perceived Doc-Man Project Organizational Structure

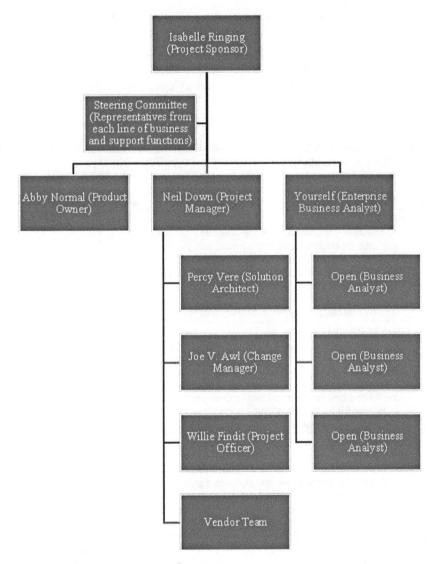

Suggested questions about organizational structure:

- Who are the members of the steering committee? Who will they have assigned to the project as subject matter experts for scope definition and then later for solution requirements and design definition?
- Why is the project sponsored by technology rather than the business?
- Automobile insurance is the largest portion of the business, does this functionally break down further and how?

- Once we know who the steering committee members are, how do they fit into the overall Blue Yonder Organizational structure?
- Is Technology seen as a function? How are the functions divided?

What stakeholders do you feel are missing?

- Steering committee members
- Subject matter experts from lines of business and functions
- Policy holders
- Agents

2. Stakeholder Register. A few are documented below, you certainly may have documented others (TBA = to be added).

Stakeholder	Job Position/Role	Dept.	Bldg.	Email	Phone#
Isabelle Ringing	Doc-Man Project Sponsor ECM Manager—accountable for the effective and efficient design, build, deployment, and maintenance of enterprise content management platforms globally to support business productivity and effectiveness in alignment with the overall technology strategy. Isabelle is responsible for leading and developing the ECM Platforms team.	TBA	TBA	TBA	TBA
Abby Normal	Doc-Man Product Owner Content Management Supervisor—accountable for the integration of strong Enterprise Content Management Platform outcomes including integration with Enterprise Applications, Business Applications, and the Technology Partnership team to drive positive outcomes for the business. Abby is responsible for leading and developing the ECM team.	TBA	TBA	TBA	TBA
Eileen Sideways	Doc-Man Subject Matter Expert on Document Governance Document Governance Supervisor—accountable for ECM policies, procedures, and document processes to ensure they are efficient, effective, and market leading in alignment with the overall technology strategy. Eileen is responsible for leading and developing the ECM Document Governance team.	TBA	TBA	TBA	TBA
Saul Goodmate	Doc-Man Involvement? ECM Platform Delivery Specialist—accountable for the management of the ECM life cycle that includes the inception, design and delivery, and transition to the run and maintain team to support business productivity and effectiveness in alignment with ECM policy and industry best practices.	TBA	TBA	TBA	TBA

Continued

Stakeholder	Job Position/Role	Dept.	Bldg.	Email	Phone#
Anita Bath	Doc-Man Involvement? Physical Records Supervisor—accountable for the security, accessibility, and remediation of all physical records globally to support business productivity and effectiveness in alignment with ECM policy and industry best practices. Anita is responsible for leading and developing the ECM Physical Records team.	TBA	TBA	TBA	TBA
Ray Sin	Deployment Specialist—accountable for measuring the work intake for ECM and Collaboration	TBA	TBA	TBA	TBA

3. Plot of stakeholders identified:

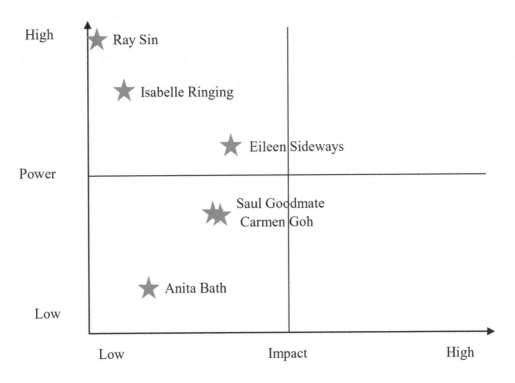

Your perception may be different; however, initial thoughts are that in this insurance company the lines of business have much more impact than Technology or Functions. Technology sponsorship is a risk that should be raised.

4. Product owner analysis:

Product Owner Assignment	Analysis of Product Owner Assignment
Represents the voice of the domain stakeholders	Abby is from the ECM domain and may not have a clear domain understanding putting the project at risk being the voice of the stakeholders.
Accountable for describing the product vision and product scope so the team understands the direction of the product	Abby has supported the ECM platforms and technology for the business making her a good candidate for product specification.
Manages stakeholder expectations by making tough decisions	Will need to do more research for stakeholders' perception of Abby and willingness to take her direction.
Maintains stakeholder relationships and communication with the stakeholders	Based on Abby's role description, she has been the main liaison between the business and technology.
Proactively manages and prioritizes the product backlog	Unknown at this time.
Communicates value proposition and business goals of the product	The last two years Abby has been a proponent for the project, but not sure if she is a proponent for the global nature of the project.
Listens and considers the team's input on backlog dependencies	Unknown at this time.
Spends time with the team and answers their questions	Unknown at this time.
Defines key product features	Abby may tend to leverage work done with the Term Life Group assuming these are the key features for the entire organization.
Defines success criteria for the product	The project brief was developed by Neil Down, hence will need to do more research to determine if Abby has this understanding to define success criteria tied to the features.
Serves as the single point of contact regarding new requirements and backlog prioritization	Unknown at this time.
Continuously refines the requirements	Unsure of the state of requirements definition and refinement from the last two years.
Responsible for the product success and ensuring the product meets the business goals	Abby has the responsibility in her organizational role to ensure the business has positive outcomes, so it seems this would come naturally for her.

You certainly should tread lightly bringing these shortcomings and questions to light. The suggestion here is to:

*   Meet with Abby and weave some of the questions and shortcomings into an informal conversation.
*   Observe Doc-Man team interactions with Abby.

- Reach out to any of Abby's direct reports to explore the business support attitude.
- Identify individuals from the lines of business and functions who interact with the ECM Group to seek understanding of perceived business context ECM possesses and attitudes toward ECM.
- Discuss findings with Isabelle Ringing.

5. Suggested business analysis RACI Matrix for Abby as product owner:

Task Responsibilities: **R = Responsible** (the person who performs the work) **A = Accountable** (the person who reviews or approves the R's work) **C = Consulted** (the person(s) who has information to help the R complete work) **I = Informed** (the person(s) who needs to be notified of the results, but not consulted)	**Product Owner—** **Abby Normal**
Approve business analysis deliverables to be delivered	C
Inspect and approve requirements (backlog item creation)	A
Request and approve changes (backlog management)	A
Impact analysis of change of scope requests	C
Approve requirements process to be used	C
Review and approve requirements traceability structure	A
Veto proposed solutions	A

6. Initial stakeholder engagement steps:

   a. Determine the level of trust between the lines of business/functions and the ECM group. Be ready to apply the trust tax or dividend. Based on past history, there is likely trust building to be done.
   b. Start thinking about the communication styles that will be used with the stakeholders in this global environment.
   c. Start thinking about the collaboration methods that will be best for the stakeholders (innovators, early adopters, early majority, late majority, and laggards)

Note: Step 3—Plan the Business Analysis Work will further flesh out the stakeholder engagement.

Chapter 3
Exercise Sample Solutions

Step 2: Understand the Business Context

1. Which of the following business drivers are present for the Doc-Man project (Quick Reference Chapter 3—Frequently Identified Business Drivers)? Write a short description of each.

   a. Customer Satisfaction/Customer Impact

   The implementation of Doc-Man seeks to reduce time for employees and agents when:

   i. Searching for, but not finding documents
   ii. Recreating documents that cannot be found
   iii. Dealing with problems and time-consuming tasks related to the use of paper

   b. Currency

   The impact to the bottom line will be mainly realized through cost reductions to include:

   i. Reduced global infrastructure and run costs of existing document management systems ($3.4 M/year)
   ii. Reduced storage costs ($1.1 M/year)
   iii. Reduced integration costs ($3.2 M/year)

   c. Compliance

   Blue Yonder is currently at risk for data leakage and requires increased support for data loss prevention and protection. This provides security for critical documents.

   d. Market Position

   With the opportunity for business process automation, our independent agents will likely make Blue Yonder their first choice of insurance provider options.

2. Based on the output of the first question, summarize your needs assessment into one or
    more Situation Statements.

Situation Statement	
The problem or opportunity of . . .	Multiple document management choices and no consistent document management approach
Has the effect on (of) . . .	Employees—loss of time searching and recreating documentation Agents—unable to locate information without Blue Yonder staff assistance Policy Holders—unable to identify the status of their policies
With the impact on (of) . . .	Employees—reduced staff productivity and bottlenecks created in processes Agents—reputation with policy holders is damaged Policy Holders—experience delays or lapses in coverage
A successful solution would . . .	Employees—reduce the enterprise risk to the organization and improve employee morale with effective processes Agents—increase confidence and loyalty to Blue Yonder Policy Holders—meet customer expectations

NOTE: A Situation Statement can be used for either identifying a problem to solve or an opportunity to exploit. The strike-through of "opportunity" is intentional to indicate that this Situation
Statement is for solving a problem.

3. Based on the Doc-Man Project Brief, develop a cost benefit analysis (quick reference—
    Chapter 3: Cost Benefit Analysis section) employing return on investment (assuming 3
    years of benefit) as the financial valuation.

    Costs are estimated at $14.88M with 30% contingency so total estimate would be $19.34M.
    Benefits are estimated for the following:

    - Infrastructure, storage, and integration costs reductions total $23.1 M ($7.7 M/year
      * 3 (years))
    - Increased productivity: a number is not being assigned to this benefit as all employ-
      ees are expected to be retrained and the change to (independent) agent productivity
      is not calculated

    Cost benefit analysis based solely on technology cost reductions: ($23.1−$19.34)/$19.34
    = 19%. Not a huge impact on the bottom line but considering the customer impact and
    enterprise risk reduction, happy to see a positive ROI.

4. Develop an informal business case to include the following elements:

    1. Executive Summary

        The purpose of the Doc-Man project is to improve Blue Yonder's capability to effec-
        tively manage its valuable documentation as an integrated enterprise. The primary
        drivers are to reduce enterprise risk and cost while increasing productivity. This will
        be achieved by ensuring a single enterprise document management platform for all

lines of business and functions. This project is essential to protect Blue Yonder from enterprise risks. The estimated $20M investment is a small price to mitigate this (unquantifiable) risk, but even with just the reduction in technology costs, the project will reap a positive ROI of 19%.

2. Background

The recent history of the Doc-Man project is summarized below:

Timing	Actions
2 years ago	The Term Life Insurance Group was made aware that their existing document management system would no longer be supported. They asked the IT group to pilot a collaboration tool as a replacement.
1 year ago	The scope was increased to include all life insurance groups and a team was formed to look at the feasibility for a company-wide document management solution. The collaboration tool pilot determined that there was too much risk in using a collaboration tool to manage documents and the decision was made to look for a more robust solution.
Presently	The scope has been increased to support a company-wide document management solution. Request for quote has been released to potential vendors and three vendors have been short-listed. The core project team has commenced.

The business drivers for a global document management approach are:

a. Customer Satisfaction/Customer Impact

The implementation of Doc-Man seeks to reduce time for employees and agents when:

i. Searching for, but not finding documents
ii. Recreating documents that cannot be found
iii. Dealing with problems and time-consuming tasks related to the use of paper

b. Currency

The impact to the bottom line will be mainly realized through costs reductions to include:

i. Reduced global infrastructure and run cost of existing document management systems ($3.4 M/year)
ii. Reduced storage costs ($1.1 M/year)
iii. Reduced integration costs ($3.2 M/year)

c. Compliance

Blue Yonder is currently at risk for data leakage and requires increased support for data loss prevention and protection. This provides security for critical documents.

d. Market Position

With the opportunity for business process automation, our independent agents will likely make Blue Yonder their first choice of insurance provider options.

3. Problem/Opportunity (Needs Assessment)

Situation Statement	
The problem or opportunity of . . .	Multiple document management choices and no consistent document management approach
Has the effect on (of) . . .	Employees—loss of time searching and recreating documentation Agents—unable to locate information without Blue Yonder staff assistance Policy Holders—unable to identify the status of their policies
With the impact on (of) . . .	Employees—reduced staff productivity and bottlenecks created in processes Agents—reputation with policy holders is damaged Policy Holders—experience delays or lapses in coverage
A successful solution would . . .	Employees—reduce the enterprise risk to the organization and improve employee morale with effective processes Agents—increase confidence and loyalty to Blue Yonder Policy Holders—meet customer expectations

4. Benefits/Desired Outcomes

The following benefits have been defined by the enterprise content management group to obtain funding for the project:

- Reduced global infrastructure and run costs of existing document management systems
- Reduced storage costs
- Reduced integration costs
- Reduced risk of data leakage and increased support for data loss prevention and protection
- Improved personal productivity savings of 885,600 days/year—assumptions based on IDC research which has identified the average information worker spends 2.4 hours/day dealing with document challenges, such as:
  - Searching for but not finding documents;
  - Recreating documents that cannot be found;
  - Dealing with problems and time-consuming tasks related to the use of paper
- Increased adoption because of a consistent global user experience
- Opportunity for automation of business processes

The 885,600 days/year personal productivity savings assumes only 30% of this study's time can be saved by half of the 82,000 users impacted by the Doc-Man Project.

5. Cost Benefit Analysis

   Cost benefit analysis based solely on technology cost reductions: ($23.1−$19.34)/$19.34 = 19%. Not a huge impact on the bottom line but considering the customer impact and enterprise risk reduction, happy to see a positive ROI.

6. Recommendation: The enterprise risks of faulty document management practices are too great to ignore and continue business as usual. The recommendation is to leverage a best-in-breed product for document management and employ a packaged solution that will conform to industry best practices and Blue Yonder policies.

5. Isabelle Ringing presents the business case to the Doc-Man Steering Committee and facilitates the force field analysis to seek validation for formal Doc-Man project funding and commencement. Isabelle Ringing signs off on the Doc-Man Business Case documented (and perhaps modified after this meeting) in question 4.

Forces for Change	Score (1–5)	Global Document Management System	Forces Against Change	Score (1–5)
Increased productivity	3		Resistance to structured tool for document management	5
Reduced technical overhead	4		Tool is too difficult to use and user practices undermine productivity gains	5
Reduced enterprise risk	5			
Total	12		**Total**	10

Chapter 4
Exercise Sample Solutions

Step 3: Plan the Business Analysis Work

Business Analysis Planning for Scope Definition

1. What business analysis approach will you utilize for developing Doc-Man scope definition and why?

    An agile business analysis approach using Scrum is adopted from the start of the project. The goal on this enterprise-wide endeavor is to define why and what is needed of the solution to allow for prioritization of the details as the solution is elaborated over the two-year expected timeline. It is expected that as change occurs and priorities change, adjustments to the scope are recognized and communicated.

2. Elicitation and collaboration plan:

Purpose	Elicitation Technique	Deliverable	Stakeholders	Estimated Dates				Actual Dates			
				Prepare	Conduct	Document	Confirm	Prepare	Conduct	Document	Confirm
Familiarize self with the Term Life User Story Workshop output	Document analysis	1) List of functionality themes 2) Update stakeholder analysis as needed	Abby Normal	1-Mar	4-Mar	6-Mar	12-Mar				
Familiarize self with the Leaders and Business Technology Partners for the lines of business and support functions	Document analysis	Update stakeholder analysis	Isabelle Ringing	1-Mar	3-Mar	4-Mar	4-Mar				

Continued

Purpose	Elicitation Technique	Deliverable	Stakeholders	Estimated Dates				Actual Dates			
				Prepare	Conduct	Document	Confirm	Prepare	Conduct	Document	Confirm
Provide awareness of Doc-Man and seek commitment for participation in Doc-Man Scope Workshop	Interviews (15)	Commitment for participation in workshops	Leaders and Business Technology Partners for the lines of business and support functions (8)	1-Mar	7-Mar	31-Mar	31-Mar				
Cross functional collaboration of the Doc-Man scope to include what is required of their document management and why.	Workshop	Prioritized scope elicitation results	Managers and SMEs representing 3 lines of business and 4 support functions	15-Mar	2-Apr	15-Apr	16-Apr				
Follow-up on outstanding items from workshop	Interviews (4)	Outstanding item resolution	Managers and SMEs representing 3 lines of business and 5 support functions as applicable to outstanding items	2-Apr	5-Apr	10-Apr	16-Apr				
Consensus of Doc-Man Scope Definition	Review	Baselined scope definition	Managers and SMEs representing 3 lines of business and 5 support functions	10-Apr	18-Apr	20-Apr	30-Apr				

3. Elicitation and collaboration level of effort estimation:

Activity	Number of Occurrences	Time Unit (in Hrs)	Total Line Item	Total Category Time
Elicitation and Collaboration: Prepare, Conduct, Confirm, Communicate, and Manage Stakeholders				
Research Techniques				
• Benchmarking and Market Analysis		4		
• Business Rules Analysis		2		
• Data Mining		3		
• Document Analysis	2	4	8	
• Interface Analysis		4		
Experiments Techniques				
• Prototyping		12		
• Observation		6		
Collaborative Based Techniques				
• Brainstorming		6		156
• Concept Modeling		4		
• Collaborative Games		6		
• Data Modeling		4		
• Focus Groups		12		
• Interviews	19	4	76	
• Lessons Learned		4		
• Mind Mapping		4		
• Process Analysis		4		
• Process Modeling		4		
• Survey/Questionnaires		12		
• Requirements Workshop	1	72	72	

4. Estimated level of effort for analyzing and documenting scope:

Activity	Number of Occurrences	Time Unit (in Hrs)	Total Line Item	Total Category Time
Requirements Analysis and Design Definition: Define Requirements Architecture, Specify and Model Requirements, Verify and Validate Requirements, Define Design Options (recommend solution), and Analyze Potential Value. *Consider Transition Requirement Development as well.*				
Establish Requirements Architecture		5		
Specify and Model Requirements				
People and Roles Modeling Techniques				
• Organizational Modeling	1	8	8	
• Roles and Permissions Matrix		12		
• Stakeholder List, Map or Personas	1	12	12	
Rationale Modeling Techniques				
• Decision Modeling		3		
• Scope Modeling	1	8	8	
• Business Model Canvas		8		
• Root Cause Analysis		4		
• Business Rules Analysis	2	5	10	
Activity Flow Modeling Techniques				
• Event-Response Tables		4		
• Process Modeling		6		
• Use Cases		6		65
• User Stories	5	1	5	
Capability Modeling Techniques				
• Business Capability Analysis		6		
• Functional Decomposition		4		
• Prototyping		6		
Data and Information Modeling Techniques				
• Data Modeling	1	4	4	
• Data Dictionary and Glossary		4		
• Data Flow Diagrams		3		
• Glossary		4		
• State Diagrams	1	6	6	
• Interface Analysis		4		
Non-Functional Requirements Analysis	2	6	12	

Continued

Activity	Number of Occurrences	Time Unit (in Hrs)	Total Line Item	Total Category Time
Compile Requirements and Design Documentation				
• Product Roadmap		6		
• Vision Document	1	6	6	
• Product Backlog		8		
• Business Requirements Document (BRD)		8		6
• Software/System Requirements Specification (SRS)		8		
• Vendor Selection documents (RFI, RFP, RFQ)		8		
• Model developed to extract packages		1		
Verification and Validation Iterative Reviews				
Verification of Requirements		2		2
Validation of Requirements	1	2	2	
Prioritization of Requirements				
Prioritization Sessions - Techniques				
• MoSCoW (Must, Should, Could, Won't)		3		
• Voting	1	3	3	6
• Timebox/Budgeting		3		
• Acceptance and Evaluation Criteria	1	3	3	

5. Business analysis communication plan:

Who (Target Audience)	What (Information Needed by the Target Audience)	When		How (Method or Channel)	By Whom (Who Provides)
		Timing	Frequency		
Abby Normal	Clarification of questions arising from document analysis of Term Life User Story Workshops	Week of March 4	1	Face-to-face interview	Business Analyst
Isabelle Ringing	Clarification of questions arising from document analysis of organizational structure for Leaders and Business Technology Partners for the lines of business and support functions	Week of March 4	1	Face-to-face interview	Business Analyst
Leaders and Business Technology Partners for the lines of business and support functions	Understanding of Doc-Man project, commitment to support scope definition activities, and provide Doc-Man Scope Definition Workshop participants.	March 7–31	2	One-on-one, face-to-face interviews	Business Analyst (Change Manager and Project Manager may attend)
Cross Functional Decision Makers from lines of business and support functions	Cross functional collaboration of the Doc-Man scope to include what is required of their document management and why.	Week of April 5	1	Two-day workshop	Business Analyst (Sponsor, Product Owner, Change Manager, and Project Manager may attend)
Cross Functional Decision Makers from lines of business and support functions	Follow-up on outstanding issues from workshop as required.	Week of April 12	~4	Group or individual interviews as required	Business Analyst
Cross Functional Decision Makers from lines of business and support functions	Doc-Man Scope Definition Consensus	Week of April 19	1	Review session	Business Analyst

6. Business analysis information governance plan:

Requirement Management Component	Description		Location	Established?
Repository	The elicitation outputs and scope definition documentation will be captured using the Office toolset to include Word, Excel, and Visio.		Doc-Man Project SharePoint site	Yes
Traceability Architecture	Traceability will be managed using a spreadsheet format and visualized in a diagram. The Doc-Man goals/objectives/benefits will be traced to the functionality themes that would be required to fulfill them.		Doc-Man Project SharePoint site	Yes
Requirement Attributes	**Unique Identifier:** Ideally, system generated identification of requirement that is never reused.	Field Values	Scope Definition Document	Yes
		Sequential Manual Assignment		
	Author: This attribute may be tracked by the tool; however, if not, this attribute provides reference for clarification if the requirement is later found to be ambiguous.	Name of Business Analyst	Scope Definition Document	Yes
	Ownership: Indicates the business owner after release to the target environment. Provides guidance on who to consult if trade-offs or negotiation are required as well.	Name of business owner	Scope Definition Document	Yes
	Source: Provides who has the authority to define the requirement. Subsequently, this source must be consulted of requirement changes and provide more information regarding the requirement if necessary or to justify the need.	Name of contributor	Scope Definition Document	Yes
	Urgency: Indicates when the requirement will be needed.	High, Medium, Low	Scope Definition Document	Yes
	Priority: Aids in analysis focus, solution selection, and allocation.	High, Medium, Low	Scope Definition Document	Yes
	Revision Number: Aids in tracking the requirement changes.	Manual Assignment	Scope Definition Document	Yes
	Status: Indicates the completion status of the requirement. Consider using values such as Proposed, Accepted, Verified, Postponed, Canceled, or Implemented.	Proposed, Accepted, Postponed, Canceled	Scope Definition Document	Yes
	Notes: Provides information that is not requirements and is intended to be used sparingly.	Free Text	Scope Definition Document	Yes

Continued

Requirement Management Component	Description	Location	Established?
Requirement Prioritization Process	The workshop will utilize some collaborative games for prioritization, which will be validated in the Scope Definition Document review.	Workshop Output and Scope Definition Document	No
Change Management Process	Any changes after the scope definition has been baselined will follow the project change management process.	Doc-Man Project SharePoint site	Yes
	Any changes after the scope definition has been baselined will utilize the project change request form.	Doc-Man Project SharePoint site	Yes
	Reference "Stakeholder Responsibilities" for change request authorization, impact analysis, and change authorization.	Doc-Man Project SharePoint site	Yes

Solution Requirements, Design Definition, and Solution Evaluation Planning Background

1. The business analysis approach will be an agile approach. The team has determined that the highest priority items on the backlog will be elaborated two sprints in advance.

2. Elicitation and collaboration plan:

Purpose	Elicitation Technique	Deliverable	Stakeholders	Estimated Dates				Actual Dates			
				Prepare	Conduct	Document	Confirm	Prepare	Conduct	Document	Confirm
Understand the current document management process for claims processing within the Term Life Insurance Group	Observation: collaborative game "The Apprentice"	As-is process	Term Life Insurance Claim Processors	15-Apr	18-Apr	20-Apr	30-Apr				
Understand the non-human actor interfaces with the current document management system for claims processing within the Term Life Insurance Group	Interface analysis	As-is process	N/A	15-Apr	16-Apr	16-Apr	30-Apr				
Decompose and Prioritize Term Life Claims Processing user stories	Story mapping in workshop format	Prioritized product backlog	Product Owner, Term Life Insurance Claim Processing SMEs	20-Apr	1-May	1-May	3-May				
Elaborate two sprints worth of user stories	Story elaboration (to include business rules analysis, data modeling, non-functional requirements analysis, process modeling, and setting acceptance criteria for all)	User stories: Ready State	Product Owner, Term Life Insurance Claim Processing SMEs	1-May	4-May	7-May	8-May				

Continued

Purpose	Elicitation Technique	Deliverable	Stakeholders	Estimated Dates				Actual Dates			
				Prepare	Conduct	Document	Confirm	Prepare	Conduct	Document	Confirm
Sprint planning readiness	Real options	Prioritized product backlog	Product Owner, Project Team	7-May	10-May	10-May	12-May				
Provide feedback on solution design and construction during solution development	Prototype	Solution design/ construction	Product Owner	Ongoing throughout sprint							
Sprint review	Acceptance and evaluation criteria	Sprint decision	Product Owner	28-May	28-May	28-May	28-May				

3. Elicitation and collaboration level of effort estimation:

Activity	Number of Occurrences	Time Unit (in Hrs)	Total Line Item	Total Category Time
Elicitation and Collaboration: Prepare, Conduct, Confirm, Communicate, and Manage Stakeholders				
Research Techniques				
• Benchmarking and Market Analysis		4		
• Business Rules Analysis		2		
• Data Mining		3		
• Document Analysis	1	4	4	
• Interface Analysis	1	4	4	
Experiments Techniques				
• Prototyping	1	12	12	
• Observation	3	6	18	
Collaborative Based Techniques				116
• Brainstorming		6		
• Concept Modeling		4		
• Collaborative Games	1	6	6	
• Data Modeling		4		
• Focus Groups		12		
• Interviews		4		
• Lessons Learned		4		
• Mind Mapping		4		
• Process Analysis		4		
• Process Modeling		4		
• Survey/Questionnaires		12		
• Requirements Workshop	1	72	72	

4. Define the activities and the estimated level of effort to analyze and document solution requirements:

Activity	Number of Occurrences	Time Unit (in Hrs)	Total Line Item	Total Category Time
Requirements Analysis and Design Definition: Define Requirements Architecture, Specify and Model Requirements, Verify and Validate Requirements, Define Design Options (recommend solution), and Analyze Potential Value. *Consider Transition Requirement Development as well.*				
Establish Requirements Architecture	1	5	5	5
Specify and Model Requirements				
People and Roles Modeling Techniques				
• Organizational Modeling		8		
• Roles and Permissions Matrix	1	12	12	
• Stakeholder List, Map or Personas	1	12	12	
Rationale Modeling Techniques				
• Decision Modeling		3		
• Scope Modeling		8		
• Business Model Canvas		8		
• Root Cause Analysis		4		
• Business Rules Analysis	3	5	15	
Activity Flow Modeling Techniques				
• Event-Response Tables		4		
• Process Modeling	5	6	30	
• Use Cases		6		131
• User Stories	10	1	10	
Capability Modeling Techniques				
• Business Capability Analysis		6		
• Functional Decomposition	1	4	4	
• Prototyping		6		
Data and Information Modeling Techniques				
• Data Modeling	1	4	4	
• Data Dictionary and Glossary	7	4	28	
• Data Flow Diagrams		3		
• Glossary		4		
• State Diagrams	1	6	6	
• Interface Analysis	1	4	4	
Non-Functional Requirements Analysis	1	6	6	

Continued

Activity	Number of Occurrences	Time Unit (in Hrs)	Total Line Item	Total Category Time
Compile Requirements and Design Documentation				
• Product Roadmap		6		
• Vision Document		6		
• Product Backlog	1	8	8	9
• Business Requirements Document (BRD)		8		
• Software/System Requirements Specification (SRS)		8		
• Vendor Selection documents (RFI, RFP, RFQ)		8		
• Model developed to extract packages	1	1	1	
Verification and Validation Iterative Reviews				
Verification of Requirements	1	2		4
Validation of Requirements	1	2	2	
Prioritization of Requirements				
Prioritization Sessions - Techniques				
• MoSCoW (Must, Should, Could, Won't)		3		
• Voting		3		3
• Timebox/Budgeting		3		
• Acceptance and Evaluation Criteria	1	3	3	

5. Estimated level of effort for solution evaluation activities:

Activity	Number of Occurrences	Time Unit (in Hrs)	Total Line Item	Total Category Time
Solution Evaluation: Measure Solution Performance, Analyze Performance Measures, Assess Solution Limitations, Assess Enterprise Limitations, and Recommend Actions to Increase Solution Value				
Assess Solution Limitations and Recommend Actions to Increase Solution Value				
Participate in assessing solution options	4	2	8	
Participate in allocating requirements to solution components/iterations	2	2	4	12
Assess Enterprise Limitations				
• Cultural Assessment	1	4	4	
• Operational or Technical Assessment	1	4	4	12
• Stakeholder Impact Analysis	1	4	4	
Measure Solution Performance and Analyze Performance Measures				
Attend test case reviews	1	2	2	
Address test inquiry/defect resolution	3	6	18	
Attend design reviews	1	2	2	
Address development inquiries	3	6	18	44
Change request impact analysis	2	2	4	
Complex implementation support		12		

6. Business analysis communication plan:

Who (Target Audience)	What (Information Needed by the Target Audience)	When		How (Method or Channel)	By Whom (Who Provides)
		Timing	Frequency		
Term Life Insurance Claim Processors (3)	Understand the current document management process for claims processing within Term Life Insurance Group	Week of April 18	1	Observation at the Claim Processor Location; BA will be your "Apprentice"	Business Analyst
Product Owner, Term Life Insurance Claim Processing SMEs	Decompose and prioritize Term Life Claims Processing user stories	Week of May 1	1	Workshop—Story Mapping	Business Analyst
Product Owner, Term Life Insurance Claim Processing SMEs	Elaborate 2 sprints worth of user stories (to include business rules analysis, data modeling, nonfunctional requirements analysis, process modeling, and setting acceptance criteria)	Week of May 1	1	Workshop—Story Elaboration	Business Analyst
Product Owner, Project Team	Sprint planning readiness	Week of May 7	1	Facilitated Session—Real Options	Business Analyst
Product Owner, Business Analyst	Provide feedback on solution design and construction during the solution development	Ongoing during sprint	~4	Prototype	Project Team
Product Owner, Term Life Insurance Claim Processing SMEs (as desired)	Sprint decision	End of sprint	1	Acceptance and Evaluation Criteria	Project Team

7. Business analysis information governance plan:

Requirement Management Component	Description		Location	Established?
Repository	A requirements management tool acquisition has been approved and will integrate with the agile project management and testing toolkit.		Doc-Man Project SharePoint Site	No
Traceability Architecture	The requirements management traceability capability will be used to trace levels of decomposition as well as tracing requirement types at the same level with one another. For example, a business rule is captured once and may be traced to multiple user stories' acceptance criteria, or a screen mock-up can be associated with a user story.		Doc-Man Project SharePoint Site	No
Requirement Attributes	**Unique Identifier:** Ideally, system generated identification of requirement that is never reused.	Field Values	Rqmts. Mgmt Tool	No
		System Generated		
	Author: This attribute may be tracked by the tool; however, if not, this attribute provides reference for clarification if the requirement is later found to be ambiguous.	System Detected	Rqmts. Mgmt Tool	No
	Ownership: Indicates the business owner after release to the target environment. Provides guidance on who to consult if trade-offs or negotiation are required as well.	Name of business owner	Rqmts. Mgmt Tool	No
	Source: Provides who has the authority to define the requirement. Subsequently, this source must be consulted of requirement changes and provide more information regarding the requirement if necessary or to justify the need.	Name of contributor	Rqmts. Mgmt Tool	No
	Cost: Associated monetary amount for implementation, maintenance, and/or those borne by others.	N/A—will be captured in project man-agement tool	N/A	N/A
	Stability: Indicates the maturity of the requirement signaling the implementation SMEs if the requirement is firm enough to begin work. This provides an indicator of requirements' doneness.	Ready, Stable, Uncertain	Rqmts. Mgmt Tool	No
	Urgency: Indicates when the requirement will be needed.	Immediate, Near Future, End of Year, Distant Future	Rqmts. Mgmt Tool	No
	Priority: Aids in analysis focus, solution selection, and allocation.	High, Medium, Low	Rqmts. Mgmt Tool	No

Continued

Requirement Management Component	Description		Location	Established?
Requirement Attributes (continued)	**Resource Assignment:** Aids in determining the resources required for elaboration of the requirement. This may include BAs, Domain SMEs, Implementation SMEs, etc.	User Story Only—BA Name	Rqmts. Mgmt Tool	No
	Revision Number: Aids in tracking the requirement changes.	System Generated	Rqmts. Mgmt Tool	No
	Complexity: Indicates the difficulty of implementation (you may use a measure such as number of interfaces, complexity of processes, or number of resources)	0 Interfaces = Low; 1–3 Interfaces = Med; 4+ Interfaces = High	Rqmts. Mgmt Tool	No
	Status: Indicates the completion status of the requirement. Consider using values such as Proposed, Accepted, Verified, Postponed, Canceled, or Implemented.	Proposed, Accepted, Verified, Postponed, Canceled, Implemented	Rqmts. Mgmt Tool	No
	Notes: Provides information that is not requirements and is intended to be used sparingly.	Text	Rqmts. Mgmt Tool	No
Requirement Prioritization Process	The product owner will be responsible for product backlog maintenance and will represent the business owners' needs.		Rqmts. Mgmt Tool	No
Change Management Process	Any changes after the scope definition has been baselined will follow the project change management process.		Doc-Man Project SharePoint site	Yes
	Any changes after the scope definition has been baselined will utilize the project change request form.		Doc-Man Project SharePoint site	Yes
	Reference "Stakeholder Responsibilities" for change request authorization, impact analysis, and change authorization.		Doc-Man Project SharePoint site	Yes

Chapter 5
Exercise Sample Solutions

Step 4: Set Initiative Scope

EXERCISE SAMPLE SOLUTIONS

1. Your response should include the Blue Yonder benefits that allowed the project to be funded to this point. The interviews should be facilitated such that each individual business leader and business technology partner has the opportunity to vet these benefits:

   - Reduced global infrastructure and run costs of existing document management systems
   - Reduced storage costs
   - Reduced integration costs
   - Reduced risk of data leakage and increased support for data loss prevention and protection
   - Personal productivity savings of 885,600 days/year—Assumptions based on IDC research which has identified the average information worker spends 2.4 hours/day dealing with document challenges such as:
     - Searching for, but not finding, documents
     - Recreating documents that cannot be found
     - Dealing with problems and time-consuming tasks related to the use of paper

     The 885,600 days/year personal productivity savings assumes only 30% of this study's time can be saved by half of the 82,000 users impacted by the Doc-Man project.
   - Consistent global user experience will increase adoption
   - Opportunity for automation of business processes

   You will be prepared for some resistance due to past history.

2. Theme visualization:

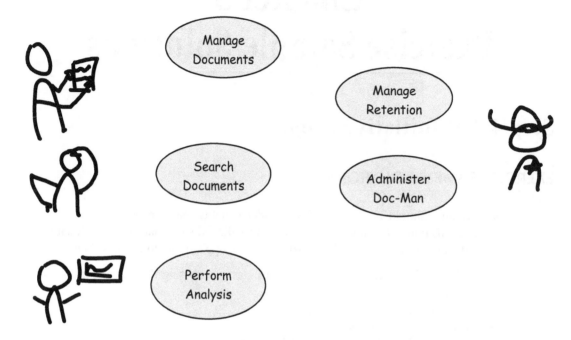

3. Workshop Planning

    - Prioritized expected Doc-Man benefits; utilize the brainstorming technique in which:

        i.   Cross functional groups write each benefit on single sheets of paper during the allotted time for free-flowing ideas
        ii. Collect ideas and post benefits; ask for clarification and remove duplicates
        iii. *Chunkify* (really technical term) the benefits (ask which benefits go together)
        iv. Name the chunks of benefits
        v.   Have the participants vote on the ideas that would provide the most benefit (number of votes allotted = number of ideas/3)

    If time allows, utilize the Product Box collaborative game technique at the end of the workshop where participants imagine that they're selling a vendor's product at a trade show, retail outlet, or public market. Participants use plain cardboard boxes, glue, paint, crayons, and other scraps and knickknacks to design a product box that they would buy. Since the landscape of the box is limited, Product Box helps identify the most valuable features of a product that will drive interest in the marketplace. This will not only provide confirmation of the prioritized benefits but will also likely highlight important nonfunctional requirements.

- Barriers for an enterprise-wide document management solution; utilize a collaborative game technique (e.g., Speedboat). A picture of a speedboat is affixed to the top center of the wall with water depths of shallow, deep, deeper, and deepest with the barriers being anchors that prevent the boat from speeding across the water. The deeper the anchor the more drag the boat experiences. Consider that Doc-Man is the speedboat and the barriers are anchors.

    i. Cross functional groups write each anchor on single sheets of paper discussing the depth of each anchor during the allotted time.
    ii. One representative from each group discusses their barriers and places on the wall at the depth their group determined. Allow for discussion of depth.

- Developing a common terminology; develop a conceptual data model by asking about information that will be critical to the Doc-Man solution. Capture on sticky notes and affix to a whiteboard. Ask for clarification as the critical data elements are identified and the note taker captures definitions. As elements are exhausted, ask for which elements logically group together. Ask which relationships will be allowed between the groupings to produce the data model. The document grouping (big business object) will have an interesting enough life that development of a Document State Diagram will be critical for consistent terminology.

- Who (human and non-human) uses a document management solution at Blue Yonder; develop a context diagram using a collaborative game of Spiderweb.

    i. Each cross-functional group receives a sheet of flip chart paper and draws the spider in the center, which represents Doc-Man, then starts to draw the actors (human and non-human) that the group expects to interact with the spider, connecting the spider and the actors to create the spider web. It is a good idea to write the data that is going across the web.
    ii. A representative from each group presents their spider web.
    iii. Facilitator will seek consensus on the most important actor interfaces.

- What they do with the solution; based on the human actors identified in Spiderweb, develop personas:

    i. Assign each group one persona to elaborate on flip chart paper. Some may feel they have more to contribute to one persona over another so encourage movement as necessary to other groups.
    ii. One representative from each group introduces their persona.

4. Workshop outputs:
   - Prioritized expected Doc-Man Benefits

Value 14	User Acceptance 20	Accuracy/ Currency 14	Collaboration 13	Process 26
Productivity driven by lower choice and discipline 8	Simple easy-to-use access 8	Single source of truth 7	Enable our vendor partners easy access to contractors 4	Information is classified: • ownership • retention • governance • use 8
Ensure safety 4	Integration across platforms 6	Avoid duplication 3	Ensure focus on operations to other areas 3	Fit for purpose metadata 7
Cost (benefits and loss productivity) 2	Mobility wins 4	The right (currency) document 3	Enable collaboration: • in assets • across assets • w/external parties • w/cross functions 3	Quality (balance between rigor and flexibility) 5
Improved productivity for all employees	Ability to know about changes 2	One place to go for any document information for all 1	Transmittals and communications 3	Reviewed process (RACI and control) 4
Appropriate resourcing	Move away from paper reliance	Knowledge	Easy access to external contractors	Standardization 2
				Security that recognizes IP (intellectual property) value

NOTE: The numbers in the boxes indicate votes that workshop participants gave to each benefit and are summarized along the top row for each category.

- Barriers to an enterprise-wide document management solution:

Speed Boat and Anchors

Phase — Deep Barrier Anchors

- Poor understanding of accountability
- System knowledge (pockets)
- Difficult to find the right information
- Lack of integration (SharePoint, SAP, Office, etc.)

Phase — Deeper Barrier Anchors

- Case for change ("not broken" at asset level)
- Change fatigue
- Overall change fatigue (lots of change globally, regionally, and at asset level)
- COTS (commercial off-the-shelf) implementation (flexibility)
- Lack of linking documentation
- Multiple and complex repositories
- No recourse/consequence for non-compliance (culture change)
- Losing momentum – comes off the radar

Phase — Still Deeper Barrier Anchors

- Not being fully considered
  - Rollout
  - Migration
  - Data cleansing
  - Retiring legacy
  - Cost/Budget
  - Implementation/Training
- Cost and complexity of migration
- Sponsorship and Leadership
  - Change and communications
  - Local ownership (buy in)
  - Culture change
- Sponsorship
  - Leadership changes over time
  - Competing priorities
  - Global system on asset users
- Not getting real global standards – too many local exceptions
  - Metadata
  - Process
  - Capture
  - Culture
- Overall network capability and capacity

Phase — Deepest Barrier Anchors

- System value not understood
- Access for contractors
- Capability of people
- Lack of/failed process
- Difficult to use
- Understanding migration of local impacts
- User uptake if system not easy/simple for ALL users

- Developing a common terminology:
  - ○ Conceptual Data Model

Conceptual Data Model

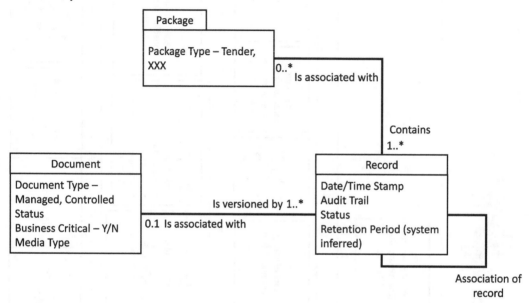

○ Document State Diagram

Document State Diagram

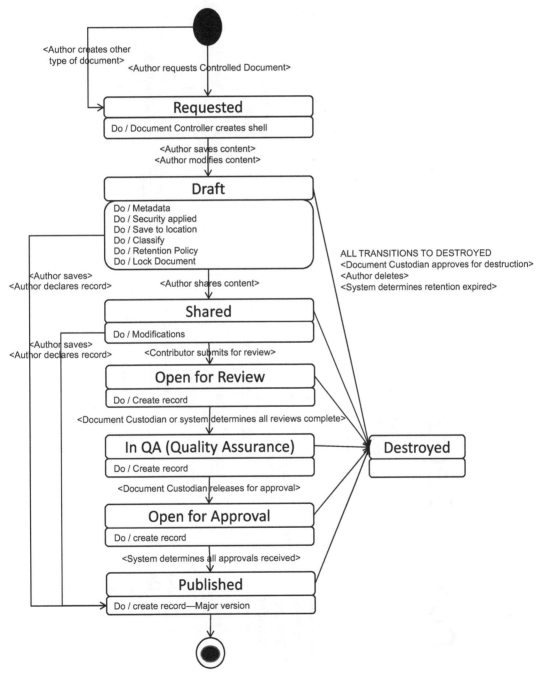

○ Context diagram from consolidated Spiderwebs

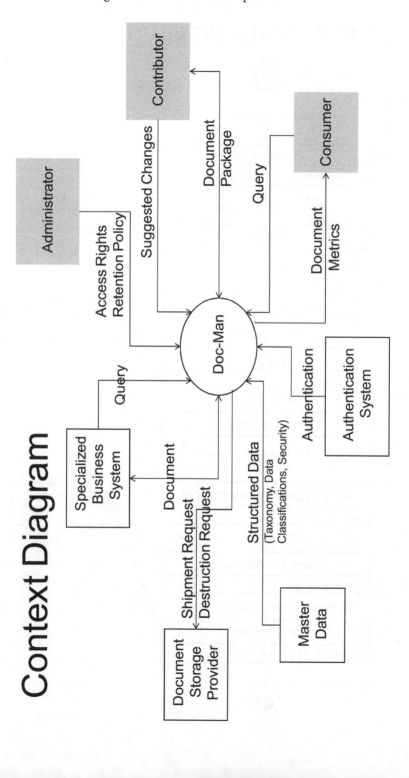

Context Diagram

- Use personas (one example for "Connie the Consumer")

QUOTE:

"Give me one way to find documents—is it really worth it to make this change?"

Name: Connie the Consumer   **Role:** Consumer

Demographics	Tech Expertise	Personal Background
Age: 53 **Children:** 3 (4 grandchildren) **Marital Status:** Married **Occupation:** Customer Relationship Manager **Years at BLUE YONDER:** 15 **Works Flex Schedule**	Low-range. Regular use of Microsoft Office, Claims Processing Suite (basics), internet, e-mail, social media	Connie takes pride in the excellent support she provides her policy holders' claims processing needs. She admittedly is not the most technically savvy user of BLUE YONDER technology support applications. There are others on the team that she relies on for help and she's not sure why these applications cannot be as easy to use as the apps on her phone. As a grandmother she is looking forward to retirement so that she can focus on her expanding family.

Needs

- To be able to quickly answer policy holders' questions
- Feel confident that I am providing the most current published documents
- Ongoing training support
- Renders documents saved across My Claims Processing application
- Renders documents saved in Doc-Man from My Claims Processing application
- Track my open claims documents

Motivations	Scenarios	Features
Accessibility of relevant information	• Search documents	• Search by claim number, policy holder name, policy number (metadata) • Fuzzy search criteria across full text • Search across relevant records of documents • Saving search templates
Track team progress on claims resolution	• Perform analysis	• Ad-hoc reporting • Canned reporting

5. Doc-Man Scope Definition. See the full Doc-Man Scope Definition Document starting on page 117.
6. Doc-Man Scope Confirmation

- Communication vehicle—utilize the Review technique and use a face-to-face session
- Provide access to the Doc-Man Scope Definition Document two business days prior to the Review
- Request participants to prepare by reviewing the document before attending the session. All participants should be prepared to contribute at least one question, comment, or suggestion as the document cannot be perfect.
- Communication for the Review:

Agenda

Doc-Man Scope Review Meeting

<Date and Time of Meeting>

Intro to Review Process: <NAME OF MODERATOR>

45 minutes for Doc-Man Scope Definition Review

15 minutes for Review Sign-off discussion to Accept, Reject, or Re-review decision

Special Notes:
Please have the document read and reviewed before attending the meeting. We will only be discussing the questions, issues, and concerns and not walking line by line through each document. Please do not read the documents for the first time at this meeting.

Doc-Man Scope Definition Document

April 30, 2019

Contents

Definitions
Version History
Endorsement/Approval History

1: Introduction
Purpose of Document
Document Audience
Reference Documentation

2: Doc-Man Purpose
Business Opportunity
Project Objectives
Vision Statement
Problem Statements

3: Benefits

4: Stakeholders
Stakeholder Classification
Personas

5: Stakeholder Requirements
5.1: Interactions Depicted by Context Diagram
5.2: Actor Generalization Diagram
5.3: Epic Stories Diagram
     5.3.1: Epic Story Briefs (Epic Story defined in Definitions)
5.4 Data Requirements
     5.4.1: Conceptual Data Model
     5.4.2: Document State Diagram (Depicts the life of a document)
5.5 Non-Functional Requirements
5.6 External Interface Requirements
5.7 Business Rules

6: Risk Register

7: Appendix A—Stakeholder Review Attendees

Definitions

Term	Definition
Actor	A human, device, or system that plays some specified role in interacting with a solution. Actors defined in this document and illustrated further in Actor Generalization Diagram and interactions in Epic Story Diagram: • Consumer—someone or something that requests to view documents. • Contributor—someone or something that inherits Consumer rights and is able to contribute documentation (Create, Read, Update, and Delete). • Owner—someone or something (include group responsibility based on system inference) that inherits Contributor rights but is the initial creator and/or owner of the document. • Reviewer—someone who inherits Contributor rights and provides review and/or endorsement of the document. • Approver—someone who inherits Contributor rights and provides approval of the document. • Document Storage Provider—someone who inherits Contributor rights to manage physical record locations. • System Administrator—someone who inherits Consumer rights and manages the configuration of the system. • Specialized Business System—something that inherits the Owner rights. • Fit for Purpose System—something that inherits Consumer rights and provides search results to human consumers in the form of document links.
Business Rule	A specific, practicable directive that is under the control of the business and that serves as a criterion for guiding behavior, shaping judgments, or making decisions.
Data Requirement	Information that is used in the system—business objects, their attributes, rules, and functions.

Continued

Term	Definition
Document States	States describe the life cycle of something important to the business (document), beginning when it first comes into existence and moving through all of the different states that the document may have. Document states defined and illustrated further in state diagram 5.2.3 include: • Created—represents the state in which the document need is being evaluated and the document components created. • In-Review—represents the state in which document reviews and endorsements occur along with the updates to the document components. • Pending Approval—represents the state in which decisions are reached on the document. • Published—represents the state in which the document is maintained and sustained. • Withdrawn—represents the state in which a document is deemed to be removed from general use and analyzed for archival. • Destroyed—represents the state in which a log is captured that the document existed and was approved for removal. • Abandon—represents the state in which the document is not deemed necessary when creating or reviewing.
Epic Story	A piece of functionality that enables a user to achieve a clearly identified business objective. Often epics are at the level of elementary business processes—a piece of work undertaken by one person at one time in one place that delivers on a specific operational objective. Epics are often a user story that is too large to fit into an iteration. Therefore, it requires story decomposition in order to break it into less-than-iteration-sized stories.
External Interface Requirement	An interaction that is outside the proposed solution. It can be another hardware system, software system, or a human interaction with which the proposed solution will interact. Describes how the system interfaces with users (UI—User Interface), another system (software-to-software and/or communication), or hardware.
Functional Requirement	A capability that a solution must have in terms of the behavior and information the solution will manage.
Non-Functional Requirement	A type of requirement that describes the performance or quality attributes a solution must meet. Non-functional requirements are usually measurable and act as constraints on the design of a solution as a whole.
Package	A grouping of documents that facilitates the ease of sharing, transmitting, and export of documents (See Conceptual Data Model for relationship of package to document).

Continued

Term	Definition
Persona	A fictional character or archetype that exemplifies the way a typical user interacts with a product. Personas are helpful when there is a desire to understand the needs held by a group or class of users.
Stakeholder	A group or individual with a relationship to the change, the need, or the solution.
Stakeholder Requirement	A description of the needs of a particular stakeholder or class of stakeholders that must be met in order to achieve the business requirements. They may serve as a bridge between business requirements and the various categories of solution requirements. Stakeholder requirements are also known as user requirements.

Version History

Date	Description of Change	Author	Version
	Continuing template population as workshops progress	Business Analyst	0.1
	Updates made after the alignment workshop	Business Analyst	1.0
	Updates of Conceptual Data Model and State Diagram based on feedback of Doc-Man team.	Business Analyst	1.37

Endorsement/Approval History

Timing	Responsibility	Responsible Parties	Confirmation
Conclusion of workshop	Review and provide feedback to Doc-Man high-level requirements workshop outputs	Workshop participants	Distribution of output and follow-up with individual participants as necessary
	Review and provide feedback to Doc-Man high-level requirements specification	Workshop participants	Feedback captured in alignment session in review log, follow-up with individual participants as necessary, distribution of finalized requirements and resolutions for review log.
	Approve the Doc-Man scope definition	Isabelle Ringing	Verbal sign-off received.

1: Introduction

Purpose of Document

The purpose of this document is to describe the high-level requirements for the scope of the enterprise-wide Document Management (Doc-Man) project, as stated within the Scope Workshop. This document provides the objectives that the system will achieve by the end of the project cycle.

The purpose of this document is:

- To gain agreement with stakeholders on the high-level business requirements
- To provide a foundation to communicate to the system vendor(s) what the solution needs to do to satisfy the needs of the customers and business
- To provide input into the next phase of this project
- To describe *what* not *how* the customer/business needs will be met by the solution

Document Audience

This scope document is intended to be used by members of the project team that will implement the required functionality of the system, as well as all of the key business stakeholders.

Reference Documentation

No	Title	Author	Location
1	Scope Workshop Output Summary	BA	https://spo.Blue_Yonder.com/sites/GRPBISDoc-Man/_layouts/15/start.aspx#/SitePages/High%20 level%20requirements.aspx
2	Doc-Man Project Brief	Neil Down	https://spo.Blue_Yonder.com/sites/GRPBISDoc-Man/_layouts/15/start.aspx#/SitePages/ About%20the%20Doc-Man%20Project.aspx
3	ECM Glossary	Eileen Sideways	https://spo.Blue_Yonder.net/sites/RIM/_layouts/15/ BLUE_YONDERB.WorkSpaces/FindDocURLByID .aspx?ID=IMRIRT7SNVXQ-11-26056

2: Doc-Man Purpose

Business Opportunity

Ensuring BLUE YONDER staff has access to quality information is fundamental to the company's ongoing success. Documents and other valuable information enable safe practice, improve productivity, and support the regulatory environment under which we operate. This project affords the opportunity to provide a single platform—one source of truth for a document and one way of working—in turn triggering an increase in productivity, compliance, and collaboration; while reducing business risk, complexity, and overall cost.

Project Objectives

The Doc-Man project has been initiated in order to achieve three key strategic objectives:

1. **Reduce enterprise risk:** Business risk (including risk of litigation) will be significantly reduced due to enhanced compliance gained through the introduction of governed processes (for example, access authorization, application of retention and disposal policies, etc.), as well as the currency of system content.

2. **Increase staff productivity:** Improve productivity of 82,000+ BLUE YONDER staff by reducing time spent finding and managing valuable information (due to easy-to-use interface, quality metadata, increased performance, and enhanced search functionality within Doc-Man and interfaced systems).

3. **Reduce cost:** Costs will be reduced due to the increase in productivity of each and every system consumer as they are able to navigate the system with confidence, ease, and speed. By eliminating redundant document management systems, support and licensing costs will be reduced.

Vision Statement

A vision statement has been created by each group of workshop participants and the outcome is summarized as:

All users must be able to easily manage the right documents, at the right time, in the right place, in the right language

Problem Statements

1)   *The problem of*   **Not being able to find a document in a timely manner, if at all, AND being able to rely on the fact that the retrieved document is the most current version is frustrating the consumers of the document management systems and significantly increases BLUE YONDER's business risk**

Affects	All consumers[1] of the document management systems, irrespective of role
The impact of which is	Growing frustration when using the systems, leading to disengagement. This causes the consumers to stop using the systems and store their documentation elsewhere (network drives, etc.), making the problem even worse. This also leads to lack of trust in the content which causes consumers to keep hard copies of the documentation in hand.
A successful solution would	Be ONE interface, so there is no choice Be user-friendly (easy to navigate) Provide fit-for-purpose *search* functionality (therefore contain fit-for-purpose metadata) Be trained-out to all system consumers to help with usability Ensure all controlled documents are appropriately managed and can easily provide evidence of this

---

[1] "Consumer" defined in Definitions under "Actor"

2) **The problem of**   **Slow system performance is frustrating the consumers of the document management systems**

Affects	All consumers of the document management systems, irrespective of role
The impact of which is	Growing frustration when using the systems, leading to disengagement. At an extreme, this causes the consumers to stop using the system and store their documentation elsewhere (network drives, etc.). This may also lead to certain functionality not being used (if it is particularly slow) and therefore invoking work-arounds which may not have the best business outcome. These work-arounds are passed on to new users and the system will eventually become obsolete.
A successful solution would	Perform faster than the current document management systems (particularly with regards to key features) Be fully supported so that if slow system performance became an issue, it would be rectified within a stated and suitable time frame

3) **The problem of**   **Lack of ownership of the document management systems is leading to a lack of business support, confidence, trust, and, therefore, utilization**

Affects	All consumers (all personas) of the document management systems, irrespective of role
The impact of which is	Confusion over who to go to in order to get help when using the systems Lack of available/timely support and training when required Lack of trust in the system and its content Lack of process involving users of the system Out-of-date content Under-developed system functionality
A successful solution would	Have full ownership and be backed from the top down Be supported by champions in several locations Be fully documented with current user guides Have regular upgrades and functional releases

3:   Benefits

It is envisioned that the following business benefits will be realized upon completion (or soon thereafter) of the Doc-Man project. These benefits explain **why** the Doc-Man project is being undertaken. The workshop participants identified and prioritized the benefits expected. The pie charts represent the level of prioritization and the sub-categories of the benefits and their relative weighting within the benefit.

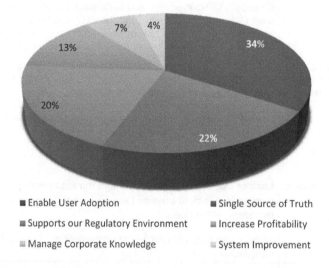

■ Enable User Adoption   ■ Single Source of Truth

■ Supports our Regulatory Environment   ■ Increase Profitability

■ Manage Corporate Knowledge   ■ System Improvement

The six prioritized benefit categories are depicted below with reference to direct correlation with problem statements:

1. **Enable User Adoption** received 34% of the votes to include:

    a. Positive user experience
    b. Accessibility enabled (external policy holders/mobile)
    c. Enterprise-wide standardization
    d. Improved processes
    e. Ongoing support

    User Adoption in general will be enabled if problem statement three was addressed.

2. **Single Source of Truth** received 22% of the votes to include:

   a. One system
   b. Enabled decision making
   c. Efficient search capability
   d. Supports sharing

   Problem statement one will be addressed by the provision of an efficient search capability as well as a single source of truth (*One System* benefit).

3. **Supports our Regulatory Environment** received 20% of the votes to include:

   a. Compliance
   b. Reduced risk
   c. Governance
   d. Quality
   e. Data security

   Problem statement three will be addressed by achieving the compliance and governance benefits.

4. **Increase BLUE YONDER Profitability** received 13% of the votes to include:

   a. Improved business efficiency
   b. Reduced system support costs

   Consumers of the system will become more efficient if problem statements one and two were addressed.

5. **Manage Corporate Knowledge** received 7% of the votes to include:

   a. Knowledge base maintained
   b. Knowledge transfer
   c. Promotes analysis

   Problem statement one will be partially addressed by ensuring corporate knowledge is maintained appropriately.

6. **System Improvement** received 4% of the votes to include:

   a. Avoid duplication
   b. Improved system conditions
   c. Increased system capabilities

   Problem statement two will be addressed by achieving improved system conditions.

4:　Stakeholders[2]

The project will only be successful if stakeholders are engaged. Engagement has been structured around the five identified levels as highlighted in the table below:

Stakeholder Classification

Stakeholder Type	Description	Engagement Classification	Membership
Executive Approvers	This stakeholder group will provide the required executive endorsement of the Doc-Man project and will be the approvers of the Doc-Man project strategy.	1	
Executive Sponsors	This stakeholder group provides the executive sponsorship of the initiative. As thought-leaders, they will proactively support the project and engage/communicate from a top-down perspective. In the initial stages, these stakeholders will assist in the identification and engagement of other stakeholder groups to ensure project objectives are achieved. They will proactively champion the cause. Key executive sponsor stakeholders will form part of the Doc-Man Project Steering Committee.	2	Doc-Man Project Steering Committee

Continued

---

[2] "Stakeholder" defined in Definitions

Stakeholder Type	Description	Engagement Classification	Membership
Change Advocates	This stakeholder group is a change advocate for the Doc-Man Project. They will not only provide proactive support in the delivery of the project, but in the early stages will play a critical role in the identification and engagement of functional requirements. Key members of this stakeholder group will form part of the Doc-Man Project Steering Committee and the Global Reference Group.	3	Doc-Man Project Steering Committee and Doc-Man Global Reference Group
Functional Representatives	This stakeholder group will champion the project and provide the necessary business expertise, knowledge, and input. Specifically, the functional representative stakeholders are the Document Controllers/Subject Matter Experts that will provide technical and business subject matter knowledge and expertise required by the Doc-Man project. Due to the large numbers within this stakeholder group, a sub-set of these stakeholders will form part of the Doc-Man Operational Reference Group. All functional representative stakeholders are change agents of the Doc-Man project.	4	Doc-Man Operational Reference Group
Stakeholders who require information only	These stakeholder groups will not play an active role in the development or implementation of the Doc-Man solution but will have a requirement over the course of the initiative to understand what is occurring and when.	FYI	N/A

Personas[3]

Name	Role	Background	Needs	Valued Features
Connie	Consumer	Connie has been with BLUE YONDER for 15 years. She takes pride in the excellent support she provides her policy holders' claims processing needs. She admittedly is not the most technically savvy user of BLUE YONDER technology support applications. There are others on the team that she relies on for help and she's not sure why these applications cannot be as easy to use as the apps on her phone. As a grandmother she is looking forward to retirement so that she can focus on her expanding family.	• To be able to quickly answer policy holders' questions • Feel confident that I am providing the most current published documents • Ongoing training support • Renders documents saved across My Claims Processing application. • Renders documents saved in Doc-Man from My Claims Processing application • Track my open claims documents	• Metadata and full text search • Provide relevant search results • Intuitive solution • Integration with Specialized Business Systems • Analytics reporting

"Give me one way to find documents – is it really worth it to make this change?"

Craig	Contributor
Amy	Owner
Spencer	Reviewer
Betsy	Approver
Jason	System Administrator

Jason the System Admin

Craig the Contributor

Amy the Owner

Betsy the Approver

Spencer the Reviewer

---

[3] "Persona" defined in Definitions

5:   Stakeholder Requirements

These stakeholder requirements[4] were derived from the scope workshops. Stakeholder requirements are imprecise by their very nature and are not intended to be used to build/configure a solution. These requirements convey the high-level needs of the stakeholders and **what** they require from the solution. The implementation of these requirements will help to realize the benefits stated above and will ultimately allow the objectives to be met.

The purpose of the subsequent visual represents the traceability between these benefits and stakeholder requirements. Most of this section is summarized in this visual. The boxes represent the Epic Stories (or chunks of functionality), with External Interface Requirements, Business Rules, Data Definitions, and Non-Functional Requirements represented below. The benefit statements have been mapped to the types of requirements containing a strong correlation. The highest benefit was Enable User Adoption at 34%. You can follow the lines representing correlated requirements needed to fulfill this benefit. The thicker the lines, the more weight they carry. With this you can see from a benefits realization perspective that Search Documents and Business Rules are going to be the most important, scoring 70 and 60 respectfully.

---

[4] "Stakeholder requirement" defined in Definitions

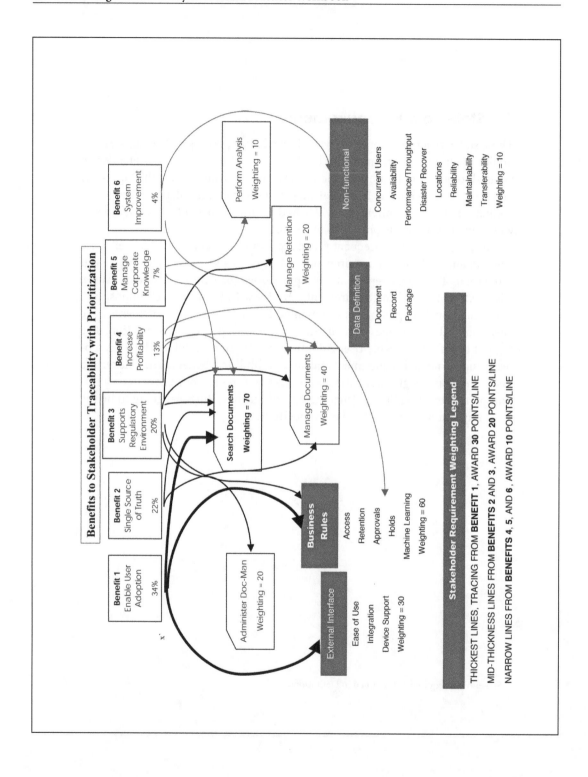

5.1 Interactions Depicted by Context Diagram

The highest-level data flow diagram is a context diagram which represents the entire system. Context diagrams show the system in its entirety as a transformation engine with actors as the source or consumer of data within scope of the project.

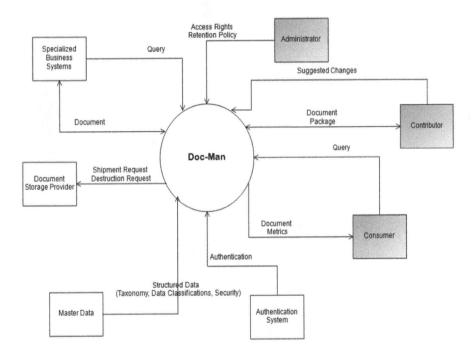

5.2 Actor Generalization Diagram[5]

("Actors" defined in Definitions section—shaded are human actors and outlined are non-human actors)

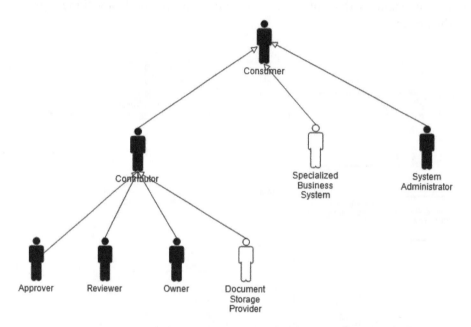

5.3 Epic Stories Diagram

Depicted in a use case diagram format, this captures the actors and their goals within the scope of the project. The primary actors on the left are seeking their goal and the participating actors on the right must engage to support goal realization. At this level, authentication is not addressed as an Epic Story.

---

[5] When several actors, as part of their roles, also play a more generalized role, this is a generalization. The specialized actors are depicted below the generalized actor. The specialized actors inherit the behavior of the generalized actor and have additional behavior unique to the specialized actor.

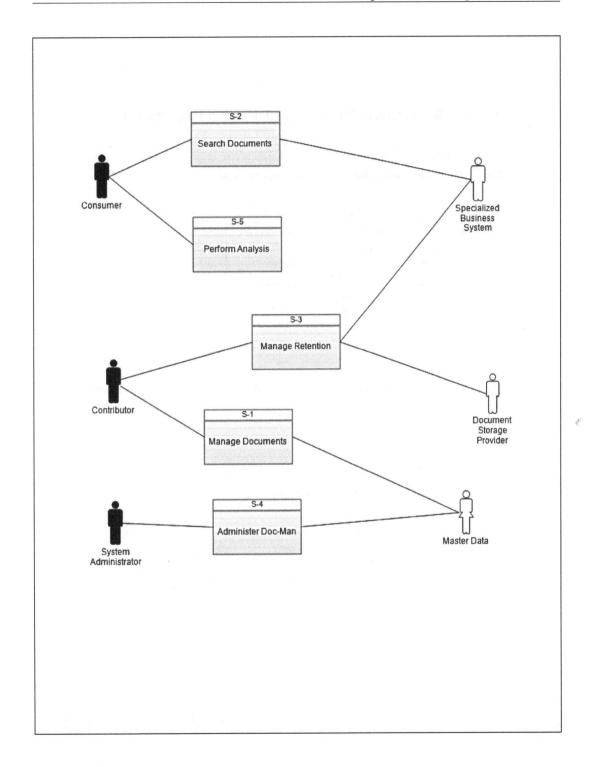

5.3.1 Epic Story Briefs ("Epic Story" defined in Definitions)

ADMINISTER SYSTEM

Administer System allows the System Administrator to:

Set-up user access	Configure error messages	Set-up notification
Set/amend user permissions	Manage retention schemes	Configure the user interface (UI)
Configure system work flows	Manage classification schemes	Configure reports
Trouble shoot	Set/amend document security	

The system will ensure:

- Adherence to system configuration
- Updates to system configuration are applied immediately within the system (unless otherwise stated)
- System Administrators only have access to such functionality, unless configured otherwise

MANAGE DOCUMENT(S)

Manage Document(s) allows the Contributor to:

Create document	Redact document	Request document(s)
Copy document	Review document	Import document(s)
Edit document	Approve document	Share document(s)
Mark-Up document	Publish document	Transmit document(s)
Export document(s)	Manage work flows	

The system will ensure:

- Metadata population (including document security and classification) is predominantly system driven with as little input from the Contributor as possible
- Unique document numbers are automatically generated upon creation of the document
- Automated workflow is used for the approval and publishing of documents, ensuring authorized parties are proactively involved in the process in a timely but flexible fashion
- Reviews of documents are scheduled as determined
- Contributors prompted (about overdue reviews) and escalations raised as necessary
- System notifications are generated when and where appropriate
- Integration into specialized business systems to enable the sharing of documents
- Version history is maintained
- Audit trail is captured

MANAGE RETENTION

Manage Retention allows the Contributor to:

Manage document retention	Store document	Retire document
Tag/untag document (for legal hold)	Manage document disposal	

The system will ensure:
- Document is safely retained for the stated retention period
- Retention can be managed both at an enterprise-level and at an organizational unit-level
- Document can be temporarily *frozen* for legal purposes (but can still be viewed)
- Document disposal is traceable, tightly managed, yet adaptable, thus necessitating all the required authorizations (where applicable)

SEARCH DOCUMENT

Search Document allows the Consumer of the system to:

Search for specific document(s) (physical and electronic)	Browse the system for documents	View documents
Save searches	Share search templates	

The system will ensure:

- Search query criteria includes all metadata and full text search
- Document retrieval based on security permissions
- Results can be filtered according to Consumer needs
- Fully integrated search across specialized business systems

PERFORM ANALYSIS

Perform Analysis allows the Consumer of the system to:

Run reports (on physical and electronic documents)	Interrogate data	View document actions (audit history)

The system will ensure:

- All document and system actions are adequately traced
- Data retrieval across specialized business systems

5.4 Data Requirements

5.4.1 Conceptual Data Model

The conceptual data model is independent of any solution or technology and can be used to represent how the business perceives its information. It can be used to help establish a consistent vocabulary describing information and relationships within that information.

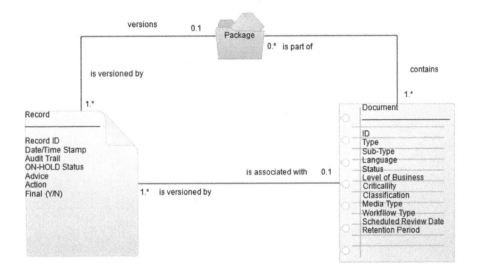

5.4.2 Document State Diagram

(Depicts the life of a document[6])

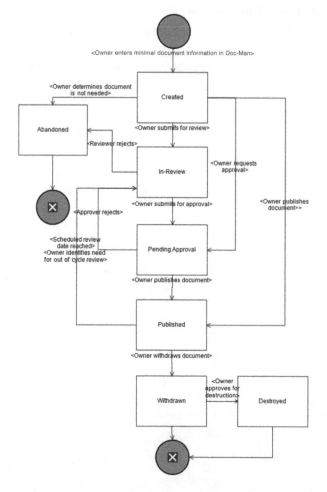

---

[6] State modeling is used to describe and analyze the possible states of an entity within a system, how the entity changes from one state to another, and what can happen to the entity when in each state. The meaning of each state can be found in Definitions.

5.5 Non-Functional Requirements

These requirements will be elaborated further and completed during the detailed requirements sessions.

The source for these requirements is the high-level requirements workshops (mainly the *benefits* exercise).

PERFORMANCE:

Response Time
The system shall respond quickly to user interactions to enable the user to perform efficiently

CAPACITY & SCALABILITY:

Concurrent Users
The system shall allow many users to log into the system at the same time so that there are no access/usage restrictions

AVAILABILITY:

The system shall always be available
The system shall be available from anywhere
Off-line access to the system shall be provided
The system must be accessible both within and outside of the BLUE YONDER network
The system must hav125e a limited amount of downtime over a specified period of time.

LOCALIZATION:

The system must be able to support both English and Spanish
The system shall allow configuration to cater for specific local variances

RELIABILITY:

The system shall be well-supported (time to fix defect, add new functionality, etc.)

RECOVERABILITY:

An IT disaster recovery plan must be in place for the new system

Back-up of system data must take place on a regular basis

OPERABILITY:

Ease of Use

The system shall be intuitive and easy to use so that the users are encouraged to use it, can learn it quickly, and have a good experience

The retrieval of documents must be simple, intuitive, yet highly effective

SECURITY:

Data Classification

The system shall protect the documents according to corporate requirements (sensitive data, physical storage. . . .)

System Access

The system shall be accessible to authorized external parties so that BLUE YONDER is able to interact more effectively and efficiently with such stakeholders

The consumer must be able to quickly access/enter the new system

The (local) system administrator must be able to easily manage access and editing permission

User permissions must be correctly set against an organizational role

Audit

The system shall provide an audit trail of all system interactions (including who accessed/amended/deleted what and when) so that the user is able to use this information to help gain insight into the state of the system content (if and when required)

The system shall provide an audit of who requested access or a change in location of all physical documents

COMPATIBILITY:

Integration

The system shall be integrated with specialized business systems to enable the user to easily navigate system content that is housed outside of Doc-Man (see Context Diagram)

5.6 External Interface Requirements

1. The system must be accessible from the following devices: desktop, laptop, tablet, and smart phone
2. The system must support the following operating systems: MacOS, Windows, Android, and iOS
3. The embedded file/folder structure (and navigation of such) must be familiar/user friendly and flexible
4. The system shall be globally accessible to all internal (to BLUE YONDER) parties unless otherwise specified

5.7 Business Rules

1. Withdrawn documents are viewable by consumers with special access
2. Definition of retention rules for documents
3. All documents that have been placed on hold must be available to the business (dependent on consumer access) to search and view (but not edit)
4. Documents that have been placed on hold cannot be disposed of (whilst on hold) due to the legal requirement to maintain these documents for the stated duration
5. All documents that are transmitted, exported, and imported must be traceable to contributors
6. Definition of compliance rules to ensure support of localized governmental mandates

7. All documents must be reviewed and re-approved periodically (depending on document type and regional variations). The following circumstances will trigger an immediate review and re-approval:

   - The document has reached the end of its validity period,
   - Significant changes in policy or procedure,
   - Legislative changes,
   - Identification of new insurance requirements or controls, or
   - Changes required due to incidents (events)

8. When there is more than one retention and disposal schedule on a document, the longer period will apply

9. The consumer will always be presented with the current published version of a document, unless otherwise stated

10. The new system must be compliant with BLUE YONDER's Information Governance

11. Any emails created from within the system must contain links to documents housed within the system, rather than attachments

12. All documents must pass through the allowable transitions of the controlled document lifecycle—see State Diagram

13. If document creator/owner is no longer associated with document, then system infers an owner assignment (solution ideas include association by organizational group)

14. If consumer's access prohibits document search retrieval, the system will limit retrieval (to be determined in solution requirements the level of retrieval)

15. Document access will be restricted by exception, leaving open access to all other documents

16. Minimal metadata is retained on documents and their associated records upon logging of destruction—see State Diagram

6:   Risk Register

The source for these risks is based on the *barriers* exercises.

ID	Description	Likelihood	Impact	Risk Response (Avoid, Reduce, Fallback, Transfer, Share, or Accept)
R4	(Effective) **standardized business processes** are not rolled-out across the organization, therefore each consumer continues to work in their own way leading to confusion and lack of system uptake	High	High	*Transfer*: The business remains responsible for the design and implementation of business process
R5	The complexity (and possible inconvenience) of the **data migration** exercise is not fully considered leading to heightened costs and extended timelines, as well as user dissatisfaction and lack of productivity	Medium	High	*Reduce*: A key component of this project is data migration and due consideration of such is underway
R7	The business is **tired of all of the change** that is currently underway and therefore is not interested in yet another project requiring their resources and time (especially as resources are hard to secure)	Medium	High	*Accept*: This risk must be accepted although it will not deter the project team from ensuring that time spent with the business is always used wisely
R13	The **single point of truth** solution is not implemented as suggested, therefore causing lack of trust in the project team and the end solution leading to disengagement and low system usage	Medium	High	*Accept*

Continued

ID	Description	Likelihood	Impact	Risk Response (Avoid, Reduce, Fallback, Transfer, Share, or Accept)
R14	The project is trying to **deliver too much** therefore not delivering anything well	Medium	High	*Reduce*: Scope and ability to deliver that scope will be re-addressed as delivery strategy has been agreed upon
R18	The business does not maintain the **currency of the information** housed within the system, therefore making the content untrustworthy and unusable	Medium	High	*Reduce*: The business is responsible for ensuring this risk does not materialize although the system will provide the capability to help prevent such situations
R21	Our **reputation** (Technology) is damaged if the project is not a success, or stalls again	Medium	High	*Reduce*: This risk should be closely monitored and kept in mind by the project team throughout. However, the team has the interests of the business at heart and will do their best to ensure a successful solution implementation
R1	The business does not have **full representation** at the workshops, requirements may be missed/misrepresented leading to lack of appropriate prioritization and continuing engagement	Medium	Medium	*Reduce*: Extensive communication and stakeholder engagement was carried out during workshop preparation

Continued

ID	Description	Likelihood	Impact	Risk Response (Avoid, Reduce, Fallback, Transfer, Share, or Accept)
R2	Clarity on the **objectives** of the project and, therefore, the **value** of the new system is **not fully understood** leading to poor uptake/usage and lack of engagement	Low	High	*Reduce*: A Change Manager has been engaged from the start of the project and is working towards ensuring that this risk is kept to a minimum. In addition, the workshops have focused on drawing out the current problems and, therefore, benefits to be gained. As the project progresses, these will continue to be reiterated, particularly through the leadership team
R3	The system is difficult to use and **not user-friendly** causing consumers to use alternative repositories	Low	High	*Reduce*: Stakeholder benefits and barriers have been captured in the workshops. These issues will remain key requirements during the execution phase
R6	Consumers (including external parties) do not have the correct **system access** to allow them to perform their role effectively	Low	High	*Reduce*: Access control will be reflected as dictated by the business and will be balanced with data protection requirements
R9	Consumers are not properly/ **consistently informed** throughout the life of the project leading to poor user buy-in and therefore system uptake	Low	High	*Reduce*: A Change and Communication Manager is working to keep engagement flowing. Communication within the business must come from above so the project will strive to ensure the leadership team remains fully informed

Continued

ID	Description	Likelihood	Impact	Risk Response (Avoid, Reduce, Fallback, Transfer, Share, or Accept)
R11	Content is **not cleansed** before being migrated into the new system	Low	High	*Avoid*: Data cleansing (pre-migration) is within scope of the Doc-Man project, therefore this risk cannot occur
R15	Delivery approach will be fragmented in nature leading to a **prolonged implementation** period and forcing a delay in value to the business	Low	High	*Reduce*: The delivery strategy aims to ensure business value is gleaned as soon as is possible
R16	Project **scope is too vague** leading to disengagement of stakeholders, prolonged delivery, and unclear expectations	Low	High	*Avoid*: The delivery strategy will be designed, communicated, and accepted to meet project scope defined by this document
R17	The **performance** of the system is unacceptably slow leading to its non-usage	Low	High	*Reduce*: Performance and user testing will take place before the implementation of the system. Acceptance criteria will be cited and referred to during the testing phase
R19	**Duplicate documents** remain within the system (due to differing attributes) leading to user frustration, lack of trust, and non-usage of the system	Low	High	*Reduce*: The system will make use of sophisticated functionality to help reduce the risk of duplicate documents

Continued

ID	Description	Likelihood	Impact	Risk Response (Avoid, Reduce, Fallback, Transfer, Share, or Accept)
R20	The project is **not backed (enterprise-wide) by management**, therefore downwards communication is stifled, appropriate resources are not allocated, and the project will not receive the support it requires to ensure a successful implementation and continued usage	Low	High	*Reduce*: The project has received tremendous support thus far, therefore stakeholder engagement and communication will continue in the same manner
R10	There will be a lack of ongoing **system training** meaning that over time consumers may become less confident in using the system and start to use repositories with which they are more familiar	Low	Medium	*Accept*: The project will ensure that full system training has been rolled out but once the project closes, training will be the responsibility of the business
R12	The new system is pushed on the consumers, irrespective of their acceptance (and level of **resistance to change**) or opinion of the system, leading to lack of user uptake	Low	Medium	*Accept*: If this risk is realized, it is likely to only affect a small portion of the user base
R8	The stakeholders engaged so far may not be available for the life of the project. Lack of **stakeholder continuity** could lead to misrepresented requirements and wavering commitment	Low	Low	*Accept*

Likelihood	Impact			
		Low	Medium	High
	Low	R8	R10, R12	R2, R3, R6, R9, R11, R15, R16, R17, R19, R20
	Medium		R1	R5, R7, R13, R14, R18, R21
	High			R4

7:   Appendix A: Stakeholder Review Attendees

Name of Attendee	Role of Attendee

NOTE: This blank Attendee Register is a reminder to have a record of the attendance. The review requires attendance from a Domain SME, Implementation SME, and Tester for verification and validation.

Chapter 6
Exercise Sample Solutions

Step 5: Develop Solution Requirements and Design Definition

EXERCISE SAMPLE SOLUTIONS

1. Preparation for as-is elicitation activities

   a. Observation questions: these would be specific depending on the process

      i. What data/materials/forms/software is used/produced in the process?
      ii. What rules (constraints, policies, procedures) guide the process?
      iii. What problems occur?
      iv. What are the process steps? Could these steps change?
      v. Why is this important? Can you explain why you need it to do that?
      vi. Why is this piece of the process performed?
      vii. Why is this information needed?
      viii. Why does it work this way?
      ix. Why is this important? Can you explain why you need it to do that?
      x. Why is this piece of the process performed?
      xi. Why does it work this way?
      xii. When can the process begin?
      xiii. When is the process complete?
      xiv. Does the process have to occur at that time?
      xv. Could the process happen at another time?
      xvi. Could the process be performed somewhere else?

   b. Interface analysis questions:

      i. Who participates (does it, receives output, provides input, approves)?
      ii. How often is the process performed?
      iii. How many participate?
      iv. Where is the process performed?
      v. What errors have occurred
      vi. What are the peak times?

2. Theme diagrams

   a. Search Documents:

Search Documents Theme Diagram

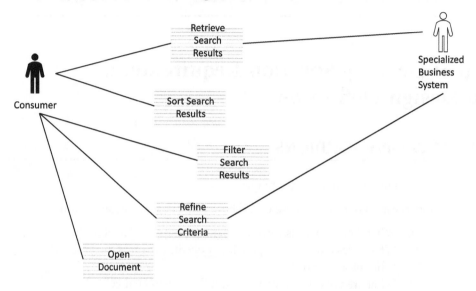

   b. Manage Documents:

Manage Documents Theme Diagram

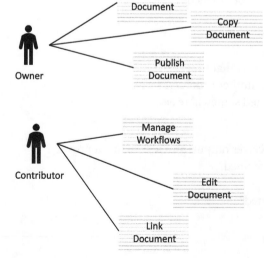

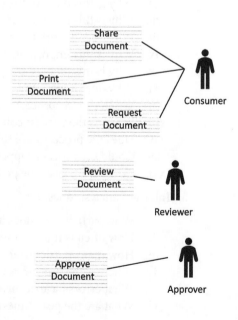

c. Manage Retention:

Manage Retention Theme Diagram

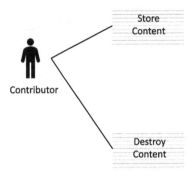

d. Administer Doc-Man:

Administer Doc-Man Theme Diagram

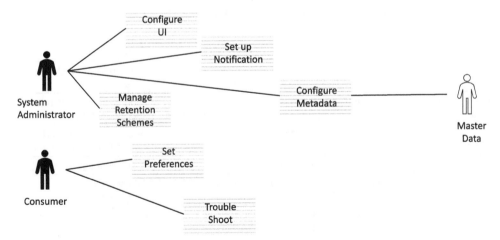

e. Perform Analysis

Perform Analysis Theme Diagram

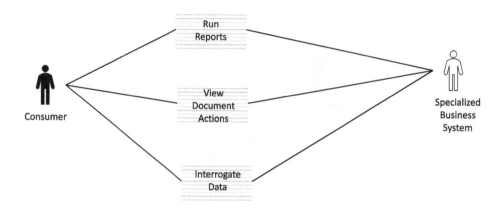

3. Elaboration of user stories

    a. Highest priority *Search Content* theme—Retrieve Search Results

    b. User story goal setting for Retrieve Search Results:

User Story Name	As a	I need to	So that . . . .
Retrieve My Documents	Consumer,	See a summary of only the documents I have created,	I can quickly identify my documents.
Retrieve Documents by Metadata	Consumer,	Retrieve documents based on document metadata search criteria,	I find all documents relevant to specific metadata.
Retrieve Document by Fuzzy Search	Consumer,	Retrieve documents based on fuzzy search criteria,	I explore all possible documents related to my area of interest.
Save My Search	Consumer,	Save my search criteria,	I can use it again.
Share My Search Results	Consumer,	Share my search results,	Others are aware of documentation.
Open Document	Consumer,	Open a document from the search results,	I can further manage the document.

c. Develop acceptance criteria for three of those user stories:

User Story Name	Acceptance Criteria
Retrieve My Documents	• Provides default tabular summary of consumer's documents • Adheres to policy for document access • Provides navigation options
Retrieve Documents by Metadata	• Populates the search facility with specific metadata • Retrieves search results for Doc-Man and Specialized Business Systems document content in a timely fashion • Provides search results in summary tabular format with acceptable availability • Prevents document access if Consumer does not have view rights • Provides navigation options
Open Document	• Allows election of edit or read-only document presentation based on user rights • Allows detection of single document match to present single document • Provides navigation options

4. Elaboration of other requirements associated with User Story Acceptance Criteria

  a. User story name—Retrieve Documents by Metadata
  b. Data definition

Data Definition Identifier DD-XX	Associated Business Object	Data Attribute	Description	Field Type	Search Criteria (Y/N)
DD-02	Document	Document Title	The name of the document	Text	Y
DD-03	Document	Document ID	Unique identifier of a document; e.g., Document Number	System Generated	Y
DD-04	Document	Document Status	The states that a document could traverse through the course of the document's life. Legal transitions are indicated on the Document State Diagram	List	Y
DD-05	Document	Document Classification	Indicates the type of document	List	Y
DD-06	Document	Security Classification	Designation of a classification to protect information during its life cycle (classification may change). Classification formalizes what constitutes business value to the organization and accords different levels of protection based on the expected damage the information might cause (e.g., Information Classification)	List	Y

Continued

Data Definition Identifier DD-XX	Associated Business Object	Data Attribute	Description	Field Type	Search Criteria (Y/N)
DD-07	Document	Vendor Reference Number	Contractor reference document identifier	Text	Y
DD-08	Document	Retention Period	Identifies the duration of time for which the information should be maintained or "retained," irrespective of format (paper, electronic, or other)	List	Y
DD-09	Document	Legal Hold Flag	Marking documents (and their associated records) to place on hold for legal discovery; an instruction to preserve all forms of relevant information when litigation is reasonably anticipated	List	Y
DD-10	Document	Source of Document	Indicates the repository in which the document resides (source of truth)	List	Y
DD-11	Document	File Size	File size is a measure of how much data a computer file contains or, alternately, how much storage it consumes	Alpha Numeric	Y
DD-12	Document	Allowable Download Formats	Indicates the file formats allowed for downloading the document	List	N
DD-13	Record	Major Version	Identifier for the snapshot of the document upon state changes	Numeric	N
DD-14	Record	Minor Version	Identifier for the snapshot of the document upon audit action	Numeric	N
DD-15	Record	Version ID	Composite of Major Version ID and Minor Version ID	Numeric	Y

c. Business rules:

Business Rule Identifier BR-XX	If . . .	Then . . .	Else (optional) . . .
BR-01	Document has multiple records	Present the published record by default	Most recent record
BR-02	Invalid metadata is entered	Present error message—"Please enter a valid <<Metadata Name>> search criteria to contain <<Field Type>>"	

AND/OR further flesh out rules in a decision matrix, state diagram, etc.

Business Rules Decision Matrix	Consumer Security Classification	Public Trust	Confidential	Secret	Top Secret
Document Security Classification					
Public		BR-03 Accessible	BR-04 Accessible	BR-05 Accessible	BR-06 Accessible
Internal Use Only		BR-07 Not Accessible	BR-08 Accessible	BR-09 Accessible	BR-10 Accessible
Confidential		BR-11 Not Accessible	BR-12 Not Accessible	BR-13 Accessible	BR-14 Accessible
Highly Confidential		BR-15 Not Accessible	BR-16 Not Accessible	BR-17 Not Accessible	BR-18 Accessible

Consumer Security Classifications are captured as columns and categorize consumers' assigned level of access to information.

Document Security Classifications are captured as rows and categorize documents based on the levels or sensitivity and secrecy of the information.

d. External interface requirements:

External Interface EI-XX	Description
EI-01	Document Summary presentation must include the following metadata: • Document/Document Title • Document/Document Status • Record/Version ID • Document/Document Classification • Document/Security Classification • Document/File Size
EI-02	Specialized Business Systems interface includes: • Email Application(s) • BLUE YONDER ERP Solution Suites • BLUE YONDER Collaborative Workspaces
EI-03	

Allowable Navigation Options from Search Results

S-2.1 Retrieve Search Results

S-1 Manage Documents

S-3 Manage Retention

S-2.2 Filter Search Results

S-2.3 Sort Search Results

S-2.4 Refine Search Criteria

S-2.5 Open Document

e. Non-Functional requirements:

Nonfunctional Identifier NFR-XX	Description
NFR-01	The system shall render search results within 3 seconds of search criteria submission.
NFR-02	The system shall provide 99.999% availability except for 2-hour maintenance window between 1:00am and 3:00am Central Standard Time on the second Sunday of each month.

5. Real options:

In reviewing the Retrieve Documents by Metadata user story there were a couple of options we could keep open with this first release.

- Keep the following options open by:
  - Splitting the user stories to separate the interface with Specialized Business Systems
  - Splitting the user stories by Document Security Classification Types

- Commit to the user story of **Retrieve Documents by Metadata:**

Acceptance Criteria	Traced Requirements			
	Data Definition	Business Rules	External Interface	Non-functional
Populate the search facility with specific metadata	DD-02–DD-11, DD-14	BR-02		
Retrieve search results for Doc-Man document content in a timely fashion		BR-03–BR-06		NFR-01
Provide search results in summary tabular format with acceptable availability			EI-01	NFR-02
Provide navigation options			EI-03	

Chapter 7
Exercise Sample Solutions

Step 6: Manage Scope

EXERCISE SAMPLE SOLUTIONS

1. Verification or validation first and why?

   Verification should be done first. Validation work can start before completing requirements verification, but validation of requirements cannot finish before the requirements are completely verified. By performing verification first, the business analyst is confident that business analysis information being presented for validation is feasible. For instance, if I ask the business domain subject matter expert if this solution requirement is correct—"The system is fast"—before verification, I will be revisiting this requirement with them again to say that was not specific enough: "How fast is fast?"

2. Verify user story based on INVEST Principle

User Story Name	As a	I need to		So that	
Retrieve Documents by Metadata	Consumer	Retrieve documents based on document metadata search criteria,		I find all documents relevant to specific metadata.	
			Traced Requirements		
Acceptance Criteria		**Data Definition**	**Business Rules**	**External Interface**	**Non-functional**
Populate the search facility with specific metadata		DD-02–DD-11, DD-14	BR-02		
Retrieve search results for Doc-Man document content in a timely fashion			BR-03–BR-06		NFR-01
Provide search results in summary tabular format with acceptable availability				EI-01	NFR-02
Provide navigation options				EI-03	
Principle	**Definition**			**Findings (Pass/Fail)**	
Independent	Documented to stand alone of user story delivery order by avoiding dependencies between user stories.			Pass	

Continued

Principle	Definition	Findings (Pass/Fail)
Negotiable	Documented with flexible scope regarding content, priority, form, intent, and function.	Pass—it is documented in Chapter 6 that this story could be split in two different ways.
Valuable	Defined features and functions that will benefit the business. This significance is known by all stakeholders.	Pass—identified in the value statement "So that . . ."
Estimable	Clearly and concisely defines the user story to create valid estimates or discussions. These discussions help lead to valid sizing and complexity of the user story.	Fail—there may be some expectations of document retrieval outside of Doc-Man. Need to reference Context Diagram.
Small	Documented to be implemented within a single sprint or iteration.	Pass—conversations indicate this is standard COTS functionality.
Testable	Derived from acceptance criteria to be independently verified.	Fail—acceptance criteria does not indicate security rights.

3. Changing user rights—Looking back at the organizational structure, we (Abby and I) should call a meeting with Eileen Sideways to determine if there is any impact to the documented business rules:

Business Rules Decision Matrix	Consumer Security Classification	Public Trust	Confidential	Secret	Top Secret
Document Security Classification					
Public		BR-03 Accessible	BR-04 Accessible	BR-05 Accessible	BR-06 Accessible
Internal Use Only		BR-07 Not Accessible	BR-08 Accessible	BR-09 Accessible	BR-10 Accessible
Confidential		BR-11 Not Accessible	BR-12 Not Accessible	BR-13 Accessible	BR-14 Accessible
Highly Confidential		BR-15 Not Accessible	BR-16 Not Accessible	BR-17 Not Accessible	BR-18 Accessible

Consumer Security Classifications are captured as columns and categorize consumers' assigned level of access to information.

Document Security Classifications are captured as rows and categorize documents based on the levels or sensitivity and secrecy of the information.

If there are changes, meet with Percy and vendor lead to ensure the COTS supports the change. Enter and prioritize appropriately a backlog item to correct any changes.

4. Recommend solutions—You should perform an impact analysis and cost benefit analysis between the two solutions. In this case consider the user impact reduction for 60% of users remaining on a familiar solution. Sample depiction of impact analysis and considerations:

User Impact Costs Output

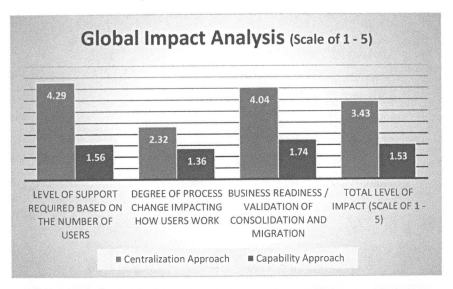

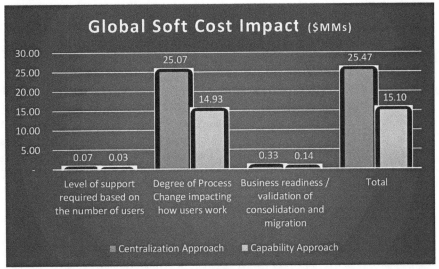

The following chart helps better reflect the timing of the proposed gains:

Both approaches assume the same benefit. However, the speed to deliver and start realizing benefits as well as incurring costs varies. This is based on the asset and function rollout strategies of the two approaches.

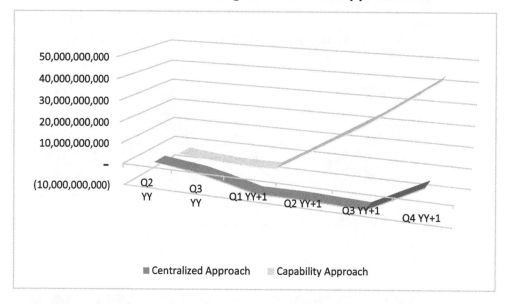

5. Monitoring of requirements and solution design—Capture an image and add it to the requirements tool as an external interface requirement. Ensure you appropriately trace this information to any applicable user story(ies).

6. Scope change—For any COTS solution, there are configuration requirements (transition requirements) that are specific to the tool. These will likely be discarded with the application change. The traceability to downstream work products will need to be evaluated for change. The business case will need to be revisited for the cost benefit analysis; adjusting the cost as needed and recommended solution. The business, stakeholder, and solution requirements should not require modification solely based on the application change.

Chapter 8
Exercise Sample Solutions

Step 7: Evaluate the Solution

EXERCISE SAMPLE SOLUTIONS

1. Provide solution design feedback—Reiterating that there is no one right solution to the exercise, here are some suggestions, all of which involve working closely with Abby, Percy, and Soledad:

    a. Utilize benchmarking and market analysis to understand how other solutions for highly regulated industries handle the interface of collaborative workspaces and a safe document management solution.

    b. Perform document analysis, interface analysis, and interviews to understand the breadth and volume of the BLUE YONDER collaborative workspaces.

    c. Perform root cause analysis to ensure that the problem can be stated succinctly and determine contributing causes to the problem.

    d. Employ real options to determine what options we have and the *last responsible moment* a decision is needed on the technical design definition.

    e. Utilize specification by example to provide concrete examples that may introduce guidance for when a document is critical to the business and must be managed.

2. Requirement allocation support—This question presents a situation that we may not be used to encountering. Many times, the BA is asked by solution stakeholders regarding what application or layer of the application should realize a requirement. For this Workbook question, the vendor's solution will provide search results based on the users' context *as long as* the user provides it as part of the search criteria. Suggestions below:

    a. Utilize risk analysis and management to determine how to approach this risk.

    b. Conduct an interview with the project team to explore viable options combined with estimation techniques to understand the cost.

    c. Assist Abby in engaging the workshop champions (from the scope workshop) to validate the business context and business need.

3. Solution team support—The team member is likely to demo the functionality, seeking validation on data elements and usability feedback from the product owner and yourself.

4. Solution team support—In an agile framework, completeness may be relative based on who you ask. The suggestion is to use the *definition of done* technique to ensure there are no surprises at the end of each sprint.

5. Monitor and evaluate the solution:

   a. Solution value measurement suggestions include:

      i.   Metrics and key performance indicators (KPIs)
      ii. Non-functional requirements analysis
      iii. Gap analysis
      iv. Process analysis
      v.   Observation
      vi. Survey or questionnaire

   b. Suggestions for monitoring opportunities for improvement include:

      i.   Benchmarking and market analysis
      ii. Business value definition
      iii. Financial analysis/valuation techniques
      iv. Lessons learned
      v.   Process analysis